"Building high-trust relationships is the foundation of effective leadership. With typical Blanchard brilliance, *Trust Works!* demystifies the and identifies the core behavi restore it."

—Jim Irvine, manager of talent manag organizational learning at Nissan North America and coauthor of *Your Resume Sucks!*

"In life and particularly in management, trust is critical. Simple, clear, and focused, *Trust Works!* is full of practical ideas that can immediately be applied to boost morale and productivity. A must-read for every manager."

—Lisa Doyle, vice president of learning and development, Lowe's Companies, Inc.

"Ken and his coauthors lead us on a skillful journey of understanding how, whom, and why we learn to trust. *Trust Works!* is an essential teaching for anyone seeking to deepen their best work in the good soil of sustainable, trustworthy, road-tested wisdom."

—Rev. Wayne Muller, founder of the Institute of the Southwest and bestselling author of *Sabbath* and *A Life of Being, Having, and Doing Enough*

Trust Works!

Also by Ken Blanchard

GREAT LEADERS GROW (with Mark Miller), 2012

LEAD WITH LUV (with Colleen Barrett), 2011

WHO KILLED CHANGE? (with John Britt, Judd Hoekstra, and Pat Zigarmi), 2009

HELPING PEOPLE WIN AT WORK (with Garry Ridge), 2009

THE ONE MINUTE ENTREPRENEUR (with Don Hutson and Ethan Willis), 2008

THE 4TH SECRET OF THE ONE MINUTE MANAGER
(with Margret McBride), 2008

LEAD LIKE JESUS (with Phil Hodges), 2007

LEADING AT A HIGHER LEVEL (with the Founding Associates and Consulting
Partners of The Ken Blanchard Companies), 2007

KNOW CAN DO (with Paul Meyer and Dick Ruhe), 2007

THE ON-TIME, ON-TARGET MANAGER (with Steve Gottry), 2004

SELF LEADERSHIP AND THE ONE MINUTE MANAGER (with Susan Fowler and
Laurence Hawkins), 2005

ONE SOLITARY LIFE, 2005

THE SECRET (with Mark Miller), 2004

CUSTOMER MANIA! (with David Novak and Jim Ballard), 2004

THE LEADERSHIP PILL (with Mark Muchnick), 2003

FULL STEAM AHEAD! (with Jesse Stoner), 2003

THE SERVANT LEADER (with Phil Hodges), 2003

ZAP THE GAPS! (with Dana Robinson and Jim Robinson), 2002

WHALE DONE! (with Thad Lacinak, Chuck Tompkins, and Jim Ballard), 2002

THE GENEROSITY FACTOR (with Truett Cathy), 2002

HIGH FIVE! (with Sheldon Bowles, Donald Carew, and Eunice Parisi-Carew), 2001

MANAGEMENT OF ORGANIZATIONAL BEHAVIOR (with Paul Hersey),
8th edition, 2000

BIG BUCKS! (with Sheldon Bowles), 2000

THE ONE MINUTE MANAGER BALANCES WORK AND LIFE
(with Dee Edington and Marjorie Blanchard), 1999

THE ONE MINUTE GOLFER, 1999

THE 3 KEYS TO EMPOWERMENT (with John Carlos and Alan Randolph), 1999

LEADERSHIP BY THE BOOK (with Bill Hybels and Phil Hodges), 1999

THE HEART OF A LEADER, 1999

GUNG HO! (with Sheldon Bowles), 1998

MISSION POSSIBLE (with Terry Waghorn), 1996

EMPOWERMENT TAKES MORE THAN A MINUTE (with John Carlos and
Alan Randolph), 1996

EVERYONE'S A COACH (with Don Shula), 1995

RAVING FANS (with Sheldon Bowles), 1993

THE ONE MINUTE MANAGER BUILDS HIGH PERFORMING TEAMS
(with Don Carew and Eunice Parisi-Carew), 1990

THE ONE MINUTE MANAGER MEETS THE MONKEY (with William Oncken, Jr.,
and Hal Burrows), 1989

THE POWER OF ETHICAL MANAGEMENT (with Norman Vincent Peale), 1988

THE ONE MINUTE MANAGER GETS FIT (with D. W. Edington and
Marjorie Blanchard), 1986

LEADERSHIP AND THE ONE MINUTE MANAGER (with Patricia Zigarmi and
Drea Zigarmi), 1985

PUTTING THE ONE MINUTE MANAGER TO WORK (with Robert Lorber), 1984

THE ONE MINUTE MANAGER (with Spencer Johnson), 1982

Trust Works!

Four Keys to Building Lasting Relationships

Ken Blanchard
Cynthia Olmstead
Martha Lawrence

wm

WILLIAM MORROW
An Imprint of HarperCollins*Publishers*

HarperCollins books may be purchased for educational, business, or sales promotional use. For information please write: Special Markets Department, HarperCollins Publishers, 10 East 53rd Street, New York, NY 10022.

FIRST EDITION

Library of Congress Cataloging-in-Publication Data has been applied for.

ISBN 978-0-06-220598-8

13 14 15 16 17 DIX/RRD 10 9 8 7 6 5 4 3 2 1

Contents

Introduction

by Cynthia Olmstead
Creator of TrustWorks!™

As an organizational change consultant, I help business leaders identify where they are heading, work with them to build a strategic plan, and bring the rest of the organization into alignment so that everyone is pulling together to accomplish shared goals. Some organizations find this an arduous process fraught with setbacks and sometimes even failure. Other organizations are able to implement the changes quickly and move the process along smoothly.

A few years ago I began to wonder: Why were some companies successful in implementing change while others were not? Was it the leadership? If so, what was the key factor that allowed some leaders to get people to work together to bring about the desired changes, while others failed?

Somewhere flying over Kansas on one of my many trips from the West Coast to the East, a lightbulb came on: this key factor was *trust*. But what is trust? How do we describe it? Does trust mean the same thing to you as it does to me? If not, how can we talk about it?

To begin answering those questions, I started asking people in my sessions what symbol they would use to represent trust. People came up with an assortment of answers: a heart, a newborn baby, a handshake, a wedding ring, a cross, the American flag. The reactions to these symbols varied wildly. Some said, "I just went through a divorce, so wedding rings don't mean trust to me." Or "The flag isn't seen as a trust symbol to people in some parts of the world."

It became evident to me that trust means different things to different people based on their experiences. This begged the question: How could we ever talk about and resolve trust issues if we were seeing them only through our own lenses? Clearly, we needed a common framework, a model that created a mutual language for trust.

I began an intensive search for that, and along the way I found some interesting academic research with sophisticated models. But they were too complicated to use at all levels of an organization, from the C suite to the front line. After six years of research—including market analysis and focus groups with CEOs, managers, and associates—I became convinced that trust was something that grew when certain behaviors were present. But which behaviors?

Working from the premise that trust is based on behaviors, I set up flip charts in my office so that during discussions with clients, colleagues, and friends I could document behaviors they thought would either build or erode trust. As the lists grew long, I realized that the behaviors fell into four main groups: *Able* (demonstrate competence), *Believable* (act with integrity), *Connected* (care about others), and *Dependable* (maintain credibility). Thus the ABCD Trust Model™ was born!

Our intention in writing this book is to raise your awareness about the trust issues in your life as well as give you the language and tools to resolve them. Our hope is that you will use what you learn to build productive, joyful relationships—and that you'll share what you learn with others, so they can do the same.

Some Perspective Before You Read This Story

by Ken Blanchard
Coauthor of The One Minute Manager® *and* Leading at a Higher Level

Trust is a delicate thing. It takes a long time to build, yet you can blow it in a matter of minutes. All it takes is one incident of behaving inconsistently with what someone considers trustworthy behavior for that person to pull away from you.

These days there's a lot of talk about trust and even more talk about the lack of it. But people need to see trust in action more than they need to hear about it. In other words, your walk is more important than your talk. As Cindy pointed out in her introduction, this is where the tricky part comes in, because:

Trust is in the eye of the beholder.

What does that mean? It means that you can be completely unaware that your behavior is eroding the trust of those around you. What looks like fine behavior to you could make your friend, spouse, boss, employee, or constituent downright wary.

Because we see trust behaviors through our own filters, we need to have a common language for trust so we can talk together about what it is and what it isn't. We have created the ABCD Trust Model™ to give you a way to begin having conversations about trust, not only in the business arena, but also in your personal life.

Ever since I wrote *The One Minute Manager* with Spencer Johnson and helped him in his writing of *Who Moved My Cheese?*, I have found that writing parables is the best way for me to live one of my missions in life, which is to be "a loving teacher and example of simple truths who helps myself and others to live more effective lives." That's why the first part of this book is a parable about how the lack of trust between a cat and a dog threatens the tranquillity of an animal-friendly family.

A story about a cat and a dog—is this meant to be a children's book? No. While you can share the parable with your kids to start a dialogue about trust, the story is intended for adults. In fact, we hope you'll see a bit of yourself—and some humans you know—in the story of Woof and Whiskers.

After reading the parable, you'll be ready to review the trust-building resources in Part II. Here's where you'll learn to assess your strengths and weaknesses in the area of trust. You'll find out about Trust Boosters and Trust Busters. You'll also see how the ABCD Trust Model™ applies to real-life situations and learn the challenging art of beginning conversations about trust issues. Finally, you'll discover the steps to rebuilding trust that's been damaged.

We hope you'll find the story a fun way to learn about trust. So lighten up, get in touch with your inner child, and enjoy *A Tale of Trust*.

Trust Works!

Part I

A Tale of Trust

Broken Trust

Once upon a time in the country home of Mr. and Mrs. Berryhill, there lived a cat named Whiskers and a dog named Woof. The two did not get along.

They had their reasons.

Woof's goofy personality and sloppy personal hygiene annoyed the cat.

Whiskers's snooty attitude and finicky habits alienated the dog.

Some time ago Woof got so excited he chased Whiskers up a tree. She'd never forgiven him.

A couple of times Whiskers's sharp little claws had come out. Ever since, Woof had avoided her.

Plus, it was common knowledge that cats and dogs did not get along. Both Whiskers and Woof had heard from their mothers and fathers all the horror stories of the generations-old enmity between cats and dogs.

One day Woof made the terrible mistake of accidentally stepping on Whiskers's tail. Whiskers lashed out, swiping the dog across the face. Stinging with pain, Woof snarled and snapped at the cat, who leaped toward the dining room table to escape. She didn't quite make it. Her claws sank into the tablecloth, and as she fell back, she pulled the entire table full of dishes—just set for dinner—onto the floor, where they broke with a loud crash.

That's when Mrs. Berryhill came running into the room, her toddler in her arms.

"Oh, no. What a mess!" she cried.

The toddler, Billy, began to wail—a horrible, earsplitting sound.

Next, seven-year-old Kylie dashed in. "What happened?" she cried.

Finally, Mr. Berryhill burst into the room, his face red with anger.

"That's it!" he yelled as Woof and Whiskers scurried out of the room. "If you two don't learn to get along, I'm going to get rid of you. *All* of you!"

When Mr. Berryhill said "*all* of you" he was referring to the three other animals that lived in the house: a parrot named Presley, a hamster named Harriet, and a goldfish named Wiggles. Mr. Berryhill's voice boomed, so every animal in the house heard him loud and clear. It was also evident from Mr. Berryhill's tone that this was no idle threat. He'd been annoyed by the chaos created by Woof and Whiskers for quite some time. Mr. Berryhill seemed to have reached his breaking point.

Kylie's eyes filled with tears. "No, Daddy! Please don't get rid of our animals!"

Mr. Berryhill squatted down and looked his little girl in the eye. "I don't want to get rid of them, honey, but we have to trust these animals to behave if they're going to live in our house. If they're going to fight and break our dishes, they've got to go."

"But, Daddy—" Kylie began.

"Daddy's right," said Mrs. Berryhill. "If the animals are going to be part of our family, we have to be able to depend on them."

"If they behave, can we keep them?" Kylie asked tearfully.

"Yes, but only if they stop fighting," said Mr. Berryhill.

The parrot, who was old and wise, gravely shook his head. To human ears, Presley merely began squawking. But to every animal in the house, his announcement was clear:

"All animals, meet in the living room tonight at the stroke of midnight. Your presence is mandatory. This is an emergency!"

• • •

That night as they were getting ready for bed, Mrs. Berryhill had a heart-to-heart with her husband.

"Honey, the dog and cat did make an unfortunate mess tonight. But your reaction seemed a little over the top. Is there something going on that I should know about?"

Mr. Berryhill sat down with a sigh. "Things aren't going as well at work as I had hoped. I had a meeting with my boss today and he said he wasn't sure if I was in the right position."

"What did he mean by that?"

"He said he was disappointed that I didn't seem to have the skills to get things done on my own. Said he didn't have time to do his job and mine."

"That must have really bothered you," Mrs. Berryhill said.

"No kidding," he replied. "My position has a lot of new responsibilities, and I've been working my tail off. It annoys me that he expects me to be up to speed overnight. I wish he'd spend a little time helping me identify people who can coach me if he doesn't have the time."

"Can you talk to him about that?" asked Mrs. Berryhill.

Mr. Berryhill shook his head. "It won't be easy. He says his door is always open, but to get a meeting with him is a major project in itself."

"Sounds like you and your boss have trust issues. Just like we have with our cat and dog," she added with a smile.

"Yeah, stress at work, chaos at home. I'm between a rock and a hard place!" he said with a laugh. "Thanks for listening, honey. I certainly need this weekend to decompress."

A Matter of Perception

That night the animals gathered at midnight as planned. Sitting high on his perch, Presley began the proceedings.

"The status quo cannot continue," the parrot said. "There must be peace and harmony among all of us, or there will be great sorrow for each of us."

The animals were silent. They knew that Presley spoke the truth.

"First," said the parrot, "the two of you"—here he looked at the dog and cat—"must learn to get along."

"Impossible," said Whiskers, licking her paws. "Woof simply cannot be trusted. He nearly bit my head off today!"

"You nearly clawed my eyes out today!" Woof protested.

"After you crushed my tail!" Whiskers yowled.

"I didn't mean to!" Woof cried, jumping to his feet.

Whiskers arched her back and hissed loudly.

"STOP!" squawked the parrot. "Keep it down, or we'll all be thrown out!"

"You see?" said Whiskers. "Dogs cannot be trusted. Everyone knows that. There's no point in further discussion." With that she turned and left the room.

Woof sank onto the carpet and put his head on his paws.

"I didn't mean to upset Whiskers," the dog said. "I never do. It's all a misunderstanding, I swear."

Harriet the hamster, who had been silently running on her wheel, spoke up.

"Misunderstanding or not, we're all going to get kicked out of here if you two can't get along."

Woof looked to the parrot. "How can I get along with Whiskers when she won't even try to trust me?" he implored.

The parrot closed his eyes, going deep within for the answer. When at last he opened his eyes again, he said:

"Trust is a matter of perception."

"What do you mean?" asked Woof.

"I mean that what looks like perfectly acceptable behavior to you makes Whiskers wary—and vice versa. For example, Woof, when you think about the word *trust*, who or what comes to mind?"

The dog thought for a moment.

"I think about Kylie, because she puts food in my bowl every evening."

The parrot turned to the hamster. "Do you associate Kylie with trustworthiness?" he asked.

"Heavens, no!" said Harriet. "The last time Kylie played with me she tried to put me in doll's clothing! I associate trust with Mrs. Berryhill, who fills my water and cleans my cage when Kylie forgets to."

"So you see," said the parrot to the dog, "trust means different things to different people. If you and Whiskers are going to get along, you're going to have to find out how to earn each other's trust."

"What do you think I can say to earn Whiskers's trust?" Woof asked.

The parrot pondered the dog's question for a moment.

"Once you've lost someone's trust, it takes time to earn it back," said the parrot. "You must demonstrate you are trustworthy not only through your words but also through your actions."

"What kind of actions?" asked the dog.

"Actions that show you've mastered the ABCDs of trust," said the parrot.

"ABCDs?" said Wiggles, who until now had been swimming silently in his bowl. "That's certainly a mouthful."

"It is," said the parrot. "But trust can't be defined easily with a simple phrase. And it isn't something you can earn overnight. You'll have to begin at the beginning and go from there."

"Okay," said the dog, "where do I begin?"

"First, you must show Whiskers that you are *Able*," the parrot replied.

"What do you mean by *Able*?" asked the dog.

"That means showing Whiskers you have the know-how to help her," said the parrot. "If she has a problem, help her solve it! If she wants results, deliver them. If you are *Able*, step up and contribute. Show her you're worthy!"

When you demonstrate competence and skills, you are ABLE, which builds trust.

Below are some statements about your **ability.** Think about your behaviors in a specific role—at home as a parent, spouse, sibling, roommate, or friend; at work as a manager or individual contributor; or in the community as a leader or volunteer. In this role, how often do you behave in each of the listed ways? Circle one response that best describes your behavior.

H—Hardly ever
S—Sometimes
O—Often
V—Very often
A—Always

1. Get quality results   H S O V A
2. Solve problems   H S O V A
3. Am highly skilled   H S O V A
4. Am good at what I do   H S O V A
5. Have relevant experience   H S O V A
6. Use my skills to assist others H S O V A
7. Strive to be the best at what I do H S O V A

Ready and Able

The next day was a midsummer scorcher. After lunch, the humans gathered in the backyard. Mr. and Mrs. Berryhill sat with Billy in the shade while Kylie splashed in the pool.

"Can Billy come in the water and play with me?" Kylie asked.

"No, Kylie," said Mrs. Berryhill. "I know you mean well, but I can't really trust our little toddler playing with you in the water until he is *Able* to swim."

"When's that going to be?" asked Kylie.

"We'll get him into a swimming class soon," said her mom.

Kylie frowned. "You said that last week," she said under her breath.

• • •

As they talked, none of the humans noticed the cat, who was walking along the fence searching for an exit. Woof saw this as a perfect opportunity to win Whiskers's trust by showing her that he was *Able* to help her solve problems. He approached the cat, keeping a respectful distance.

"Whiskers," he said, "I noticed that you have been trying to find a way through the backyard fence for a long time."

"Yes," said the cat. "Unless I want to walk all the way around the house and out the front yard, I have to climb the backyard fence and jump over."

"I am going to make it easier for you to come and go," said Woof.

The cat looked at the dog, blinked, and then opened her mouth wide in a big yawn.

"Uh-huh. Right. Sure you will," she said. She had heard Woof boast like this before.

"I can tell you don't have confidence in me," said the dog.

"You're right," said Whiskers. "I don't."

"That's okay," said Woof. "I'm going to do this whether you think I'm *Able* or not."

And help her he did. Later that day he went out to the fence and began digging. Soon there was a perfect little cat-sized hole for the cat to crawl through. When he finished the hole to his satisfaction, Woof searched out Whiskers, who was taking her afternoon nap.

"Excuse me. I hate to wake you, but I think you'll be excited to see the new exit I made for you under the backyard fence," said Woof.

The cat lifted her head, looked across the yard, and said, "Well, what do you know, you dug a hole. Good for you." Then she promptly went back to sleep.

But Woof was not about to give up so easily. He might have been a dog, but even he knew that anyone can do something once and not necessarily be competent. He would have to impress her again.

"Excuse me," he said to the cat. "I hate to wake you once more, but I get the feeling you're not terribly impressed."

"Bingo," said Whiskers. "If you want to impress me, bring me some catnip."

The next day Woof searched the surrounding property and found a patch of fresh catnip growing in a sunny spot among some rocks. He gathered a leafy bunch in his mouth and dropped it at Whiskers's feet.

"Very nice," said the cat, sniffing the catnip with curiosity.

"So *now* are you impressed with my ability?" Woof asked hopefully.

"Not yet," replied the cat. "After all, it could be beginner's luck. If you really want to impress me with your competence, bring me a fish."

"I know I haven't been very helpful to you in the past," said the dog, "and it's going to take a while before you trust my skills. Getting you a fish won't be easy, but I'm certainly going to give it my best effort."

• • •

On Monday when Mr. and Mrs. Berryhill got home from their busy days, they sat down together over a couple of iced teas.

"How was your day at the office?" Mr. Berryhill asked his wife.

"Busy. I was nearly late picking up the kids from day care," she replied. "How did it go today with your boss?"

"I did a lot of thinking about my situation over the weekend," Mr. Berryhill said as he stirred his tea. "I decided that no matter how difficult it was, I was determined to get an appointment to see him today."

"Did you have any luck?" Mrs. Berryhill asked.

"I sure did—right after lunch," he replied.

"How'd that go?" she asked.

"My mother always said when you're having a challenging conversation with someone, it's always best to make a lot of 'I' statements rather than 'you' statements, because nobody can argue with your feelings. So I told him, 'I want to thank you for your feedback last week. I also want to apologize for letting you down. I realized I'm taking on some new responsibilities that are stretching my skills. I know how busy you are, so is there anyone you can recommend in the company who could mentor me for a while? I'm excited about the opportunity and want to be *Able* to develop the skills required to be excellent at my job.'"

"Wow," said Mrs. Berryhill, "I'm impressed. You were really vulnerable. How did he respond?"

"I was amazed," said Mr. Berryhill. "He thanked me for my honesty and suggested two people who might be able to help. He got right on the phone and left both of them messages. He suggested we talk in a couple of weeks to check my progress. He said he trusted that the next couple of weeks would be good learning opportunities for me."

"That's terrific," said Mrs. Berryhill.

Mr. Berryhill smiled at his wife. "Your digging for what was bothering me really helped me think it through. Thanks."

• • •

It took a week, but after a steep learning curve and a great deal of effort, the dog snatched a small fish from a nearby pond and plopped it at the cat's feet.

"This smells delicious," said Whiskers, poking her nose toward the fish. "I must say, I'm beginning to be impressed."

But Woof didn't stop there. He surprised her the following day with a rubber ducky he'd plucked from the swimming pool. Later that week he brought her a mouse toy he found near the trash cans.

Finally, Whiskers said, "Thank you. I do appreciate the passageway in the fence and all the gifts you've been bringing me."

Woof was pleased and very hopeful. "Does this mean you finally think I'm *Able* to help you?"

"I suppose it does," said the cat.

"*Now* will you trust me?" asked the dog.

"Trust you? No. It's all well and good that you can dig holes and hunt for cat treasures. But just because you're able to do these things doesn't mean I can trust you. There are other issues."

"Other issues? Like what?" asked Woof.

The cat sighed and shook her sleek little head. "I don't have time to get into that. Look, cats and dogs just don't get along. It's common knowledge."

With that, she put her tail in the air and walked away, making clear that the conversation was over.

Believe It or Not

Disappointed that Whiskers didn't yet trust him, Woof sought out Presley the parrot.

"For weeks now I've been doing my best to show the cat that I'm *Able* to help her," Woof said.

"Yes, so I've heard," said Presley. "Rumor has it you've done well, so why the long face?"

Hanging his head, Woof said, "Whiskers still doesn't trust me. She says there are 'other issues.'"

The parrot nodded thoughtfully. "Don't be so discouraged, Woof," he said. "You're not going to win Whiskers's trust—and vice versa—in the blink of an eye. Building trust takes time."

"But surely there's more I can do to show Whiskers I'm trustworthy," said the dog.

"There certainly is," said the parrot. "Now that you've demonstrated you are *Able*, you must show Whiskers you are *Believable*."

"How do I do that?" Woof asked.

"You must act with integrity," said the parrot. "That means that if Whiskers tells you something in confidence, you'll keep it to yourself and not bark it all over town."

Woof was taken aback. Come to think of it, he had barked about a few of the cat's confidences over the years.

"Furthermore," said the parrot, "when you do something wrong, you must admit to it and apologize for it."

"I can do that," said Woof.

"But if you want to be *Believable,* the most important thing is to stay honest. That means no exaggerating—or minimizing—the truth."

Woof nodded, realizing that he had been known to stretch the truth a bit.

> **Building trust takes time.**

"Being honest means that if you give Whiskers your word, you have to follow through on it so she knows that the words coming from your mouth will match your behavior."

"Is there anything else I need to know about being *Believable*?" the dog asked.

"Actually, there are quite a few things you need to know," the parrot said. "When you're faced with a tough decision, be fair in your choices. Be sincere in word and deed. Avoid being judgmental. Show respect for others."

"It sounds like being *Believable* is a character issue," Woof said.

"That's right," said the parrot. "Being **Believable** isn't a simple trick you can learn, like fetching a stick. It requires looking inside at your motives."

So for the next several weeks Woof did some soul-searching. He realized that Whiskers would come to trust him only when she saw what a good dog he was, deep down. As he was searching his heart, he remembered the day he had chased Whiskers up the tree. At the time he claimed it was due to overexcitement, but now that he was being honest with himself, he admitted he'd gotten a perverse pleasure in seeing the cat be so afraid.

It was time to make amends.

• • •

When you act with integrity, you are BELIEVABLE, which builds trust.

Below are some statements about your **believability**. Thinking about the same role you chose to analyze for the ABLE area of trust, how often do you behave in each of the listed ways? Circle one response that best describes your behavior.

H—Hardly ever
S—Sometimes
O—Often
V—Very often
A—Always

1. Keep confidences   H S O V A
2. Admit when I am wrong   H S O V A
3. Am honest   H S O V A
4. Avoid talking behind people's backs   H S O V A
5. Am sincere   H S O V A
6. Am nonjudgmental   H S O V A
7. Show respect for others   H S O V A

Just about the time the parrot was telling the dog how to be *Believable,* Kylie approached her mom, who was working at her desk.

"Mom, you keep saying you're going to get Billy some swimming lessons. But you haven't, and I don't think you're ever going to do it."

Mrs. Berryhill opened her mouth to begin an excuse, but when she saw the look in Kylie's eyes, she realized she was losing her daughter's trust. It was clear her daughter didn't see her as *Believable*.

"I'm sorry, honey," she said. "You're right. I haven't set up his swimming lessons yet. Let's go to the computer. You can help me find out where they're giving lessons in the neighborhood so I can sign Billy up."

"Yay!" said Kylie. "I can't wait for him to be able to play with me in the pool."

Within a few minutes, they had found a school and enrolled Billy in a class.

• • •

The next day Woof found Whiskers stretched out on the carpet, warming her silky fur in the sunshine pouring through the window.

"Whiskers," he said, "I would like to apologize to you."

She opened her eyes ever so slightly. "What have you done now?" she asked.

"Months ago I chased you up the big oak tree in the front yard," said the dog. "Not only was that disrespectful, but I frightened you and that was wrong. I sincerely apologize and promise you I won't do that again."

Whiskers lay back and closed her eyes again. "Apology accepted," she said. "Now let me sleep."

Harriet, who had been eavesdropping on their conversation and could hardly believe her ears, stopped running on her wheel. Could it be that Woof and Whiskers were finally learning to trust each other?

Not only did Woof apologize, but over the next few weeks, he demonstrated that he was *Believable* to Whiskers in many other ways. For example, when Harriet and Wiggles were complaining about the way the cat rubbed Mrs. Berryhill's leg and got all of her attention, the dog refused to chime in.

"Whiskers is conceited and self-centered," they said. "Don't you agree, Woof?"

To this Woof responded, "She is my friend. If you two have issues with Whiskers, you really should discuss them with her."

Word of Woof's gallant response got back to Whiskers and to her great surprise, she was touched.

On a windy afternoon when Woof was feeling frisky, he succumbed to his old ways and bounded toward Whiskers at full speed. He didn't do it on purpose; it was simply the force of deeply ingrained habit. Just in time he remembered his promise not to chase her. He stopped dead in his tracks, wagged his tail in a friendly, nonthreatening way, and waited politely for her to pass by. The change of behavior took considerable effort, and Woof felt proud of himself for achieving it.

As the cat passed by, she said, "A bit windy today, isn't it?"

To herself, Whiskers thought: *Woof's not such a bad fellow after all.*

The Connection

One night when all the animals were gathered in the living room, Whiskers made an announcement.

"As you all may have noticed, things have settled down a lot between Woof and me," the cat said. "We haven't had a major fight for weeks now, and even Mr. Berryhill seems to have forgotten his annoyance with us. Harriet, you said that we were all going to get kicked out of this house unless Woof could get along with me. I'm pleased to announce that the issue has been resolved."

Whiskers walked over to Woof and sat down before him. "What I'm saying is, I think I finally trust you," she said.

Presley, who had been watching all these developments without much comment, finally spoke up.

"Not so fast," the parrot said. "Trust is a two-way street. Before we can be certain that peace will reign in this household, we must find out if the feelings are mutual." Presley turned to the dog. "Woof, do you trust Whiskers? Be honest."

Woof looked at Whiskers for a long moment. Finally, he said, "Honestly? Not really. On far too many occasions I've seen those claws come out without warning. Sorry as I am to say it, I can't state that I'm certain it won't happen again."

Whiskers looked offended. "But we're friends now! Why don't you trust me?"

"It's hard to say," said Woof, "but if I had to try, what it really amounts to is that I don't *feel* I can trust you."

The cat nonchalantly licked her coat a few times. Although she didn't show it on the outside, inside her heart was heavy. Then she looked to the parrot.

"Presley, this silly dog doesn't trust me, even though I've proclaimed my friendship," she said. "How am I supposed to make this dumb dog see the truth?"

With that slur, Woof growled under his breath, just loud enough for the hamster and goldfish

> **Trust is a two-way street.**

to hear. Then he got up and left the room. He'd had enough of the cat's insults.

"Oh dear," said Wiggles. "I can see right now that if Whiskers can't win Woof's trust, the fighting is bound to start up again."

"And we'll all get kicked out of here," said Harriet in a worried tone.

"But I have no idea how to get through Woof's thick head," said the cat.

"You can start by speaking about him with a little more respect," said the parrot with a laugh. "Woof says he doesn't feel he can trust you, right?"

"So he says," the cat replied.

"Your job, then, is to show Woof that you're **Connected** to him," said the parrot. "You must demonstrate to him through your actions that you care about him. *Do* you care about him?"

Whiskers thought about all that Woof had done for her the past several weeks—the catnip, the kitty toys, the steadfast friendship.

"Yes," she said, "I do. I was just thinking recently that he's really not a bad fellow, especially for a dog."

"Then you must show him you care," said the parrot.

"But how?" asked Whiskers.

"For one thing, show a little empathy toward him. When he does something well, praise his efforts. Show interest in his life. Do you think you can do that?"

"I suppose so," said the cat.

"At the same time," continued the parrot, "communicate with Woof. Let him get to know you better by sharing information about yourself. Listen to his opinions and points of view with an open mind. Ask for his ideas and input."

Whiskers lifted a paw and licked between her claws. "That's quite a tall order for a cat, but I'll give it a try," she said.

Connecting with others wasn't the cat's strong suit. She knew she was going to have to work hard to change her behavior.

• • •

When you care about others, you are CONNECTED, which builds trust.

Below are some statements about your **connectedness**. Thinking about the same role you chose to analyze for the ABLE and BELIEVABLE areas of trust, how often do you behave in each of the listed ways? Circle one response that best describes your behavior.

H—Hardly ever
S—Sometimes
O—Often
V—Very often
A—Always

1. Listen well   H S O V A
2. Praise others' efforts   H S O V A
3. Show interest in others   H S O V A
4. Share about myself   H S O V A
5. Work well with others   H S O V A
6. Show empathy for others   H S O V A
7. Ask for input   H S O V A

"I had a great meeting with my boss today," chimed Mr. Berryhill as he helped Mrs. Berryhill set the table for dinner.

"Really? That's great," she replied. "After that first follow-up meeting you weren't so sure things were going to work out."

"That's true, but in the past month I've gotten tremendous help from the two people my boss referred me to. I was really excited about reporting that to him at today's meeting. But he beat me to the punch."

"How so?"

"He had already gotten glowing reports from those two colleagues and was very impressed with my progress. After a rocky start, I think we're really communicating well now. We even talked about the World Series. I didn't know he was a baseball nut and he didn't know that about me, either. It was fun."

"Sounds like you're beginning to feel *Connected* to each other," said Mrs. Berryhill.

"I think we are. He seems to appreciate the fact that I went out of my way to learn new skills and follow through on what I promised to do. And I appreciate his new interest in me as a human being."

• • •

One day as Woof was sitting on the back patio, Whiskers saw an opportunity to connect. She joined him and asked about his life. She was surprised to find out he'd been adopted from an animal shelter and didn't even know his mother and father. Then she shared about her own life as the youngest kitten in a litter of six. They talked about their favorite pastimes and foods. Although Whiskers did not share Woof's passion for digging holes, she listened with interest as he described the many treasures he'd unearthed. And though she frankly found his barking irritating, she praised how well he protected the home when strangers came to the door.

It wasn't long before Whiskers was no longer trying to be *Connected* to Woof; connecting with him came naturally. The same was true for Woof. He enjoyed sharing information with Whiskers. As they continued to keep the lines of communication open, they didn't have to hope and wish for a caring relationship—the bond between them was real.

It All Depends

"The two of you have come a long way," said Presley to the dog and the cat at their next council meeting. "You've made tremendous progress on your relationship."

The others nodded in agreement.

"Woof," continued the parrot, "you've not only stopped chasing Whiskers, you've done so consistently. I think we can all rely on you to continue that good behavior and stand up for her.

"Whiskers, you've not only stopped criticizing and clawing Woof, you've also reached out to get to know him. In fact, you've really brought out the best in him."

Harriet and Wiggles heartily concurred.

"The two of you getting along has created a much more harmonious atmosphere for the rest of us," said the hamster.

"Yeah," said the goldfish. "And Mr. Berryhill hasn't threatened to kick us out lately."

"These two have set a fine example for the rest of us," said the parrot. "Through their actions and words, they have shown us how being *Able, Believable,* and *Connected* builds trust. We've seen that by using these tools, even age-old enemies like cats and dogs can get along."

"Life is good now that we've learned the ABCs of trust," said Woof with a smile.

"But we're not out of the woods yet," said the parrot. "There's one more element of trust that remains to be explored. When we've mastered this, we'll truly be trustworthy."

Whiskers, ever curious, asked, "What is this final element of trust?"

Presley replied, "As you'll remember, Mrs. Berryhill told Kylie that if we were going to stay, the humans had to be able to depend on us. That means we need to commit to working together as a team. There must be trust not just between you and Woof, but among all of us, working together. We must create a climate of trust."

"How do we do that?" asked Harriet.

"In addition to behaving in ways that show we are *Able, Believable,* and *Connected,* we need to demonstrate that we are *Dependable,*" replied the parrot, "both individually and as a team. If we can count on each other and be there for each other— and the humans—no matter what—that's when we'll know we have created a climate of trust. It's all about the way we behave."

"But how can a fish like me behave in a way that's *Dependable*?" asked Wiggles.

"It's not hard," replied the parrot. "For example, when somebody asks for help, respond on time and do what you say you will do."

"I can do that," said the goldfish.

"What about me?" asked Harriet. "How can I behave in a way that's **Dependable**?"

"Follow up," replied the parrot. "And be consistent—don't say one thing and do the other. Be organized—no more tossing your shavings outside your cage!"

"How might a feline be **Dependable**?" asked Whiskers.

"Be on time—no dawdling," said the parrot. "And hold yourself accountable rather than placing responsibility for mistakes on others."

"In other words, we all have to step up and pull our weight around here, right?" said Woof.

"Right," said Presley. "If we are dependable and work together, Mr. Berryhill and the rest of the family also will be able to depend on us."

• • •

When you maintain reliability, you are DEPENDABLE, which builds trust.

Below are some statements about your **dependability**. Thinking about the same role you chose to analyze for the ABLE, BELIEVABLE, and CONNECTED areas of trust, how often do you behave in each of the listed ways? Circle one response that best describes your behavior.

H—Hardly ever
S—Sometimes
O—Often
V—Very often
A—Always

1. Do what I say I will do	H S O V A
2. Am timely	H S O V A
3. Am responsive to requests	H S O V A
4. Am organized	H S O V A
5. Am accountable for my actions	H S O V A
6. Follow up	H S O V A
7. Am consistent	H S O V A

It was a beautiful summer evening. For several blessed weeks life had been nearly perfect. Peace and sunshine filled the house as Mr. Berryhill arrived home from work. When he walked through the door, he had exciting news.

"You won't believe what happened at work today," he said to Mrs. Berryhill. "My boss called me into his office."

"And?" she asked, raising her brows.

"First, he congratulated me on my excellent progress in my job."

"That's terrific," said Mrs. Berryhill.

"Then he told me about an opportunity that's just come up. There's a new position that he thinks will really build on my new skills as well as my natural strengths. He said he was considering another strong candidate for the job, but was offering it to me because he feels he can depend on me."

"That's great news!" said Mrs. Berryhill. "Boy, your relationship certainly has turned around."

"Yeah, trust works!" said Mr. Berryhill. "But there's a catch. The new position is in a city all the way across the country. We'd have to pack up and move by the end of the summer."

Mrs. Berryhill stood with her mouth slightly agape. "Wow, that is a catch. Is the opportunity worth it?"

"It really is, honey. I'd not only have more responsibility, but I'd also get a significant increase in pay. It's a tremendous, career-enhancing move. Are you up for it?"

"I need some time to mull this over," she said. "There's my work to think about and most important, the kids. Billy's too young to care, but the move might be a little hard on Kylie."

"I was thinking about that, especially since I don't think it makes sense to move all the animals to the city."

Mrs. Berryhill shook her head. "That's going to be a tough sell, honey," she said.

A Terrible Blow

The entire clan—Mr. and Mrs. Berryhill, Kylie, their toddler, and all the animals—was gathered in the living room after dinner that evening, enjoying the rhythmic music of crickets and the warm, sweet-scented air coming through the open windows.

Then Mr. Berryhill turned to his daughter and dropped the bomb.

"I just got an important promotion at work, Kylie. It's a new job with more responsibilities and a lot more money, so we can move into a nice new place. Plus, there will be museums and plays and all kinds of fun new things for you and Billy to do. Your mom and I have talked it over and we both agree it's a great idea."

"Yay!" said Kylie. "That sounds awesome!"

"The only problem," said Mr. Berryhill, "is that my new job is an awfully long way from here. In fact, it's all the way on the other side of the country." He reached for his iPad and brought up a map of the country. "We'll be moving all the way from here"—he pointed to their current town— "to here." He pointed to a city on the opposite side of the continent.

"Given how far we have to move, I think we're going to have to find homes for all these animals. We can't take them with us."

"But, Daddy!" Kylie cried. "The animals have been good! You promised if they were good they could stay. You can't give them away!"

Tears sprang to Kylie's eyes. Although she didn't have the words to describe it, she was questioning how *Dependable* her dad was.

"I know they've been good, but moving five animals three thousand miles is hard to do, and your dad and I already have enough work to do to make this move happen," said Mrs. Berryhill. "Besides, they probably wouldn't like the city. I promise we'll find them good homes where they can make another little girl or boy happy."

The animals sat in shocked silence. Despite all their best efforts, circumstances outside their control now threatened their peaceful lives.

• • •

That night Presley called another animal council.

"The news is terrible, it's true," the parrot said. "Just remember: no matter what happens, we're a team. That means we use all our abilities and integrity, and we stay connected to one another. Our very lives are depending on us being a team now. Right?"

"Right," all the animals said in unison.

"But how are we going to be a team when Mr. and Mrs. Berryhill are going to give us away?" the hamster said sadly.

"I don't know," said the parrot. "Let's just trust each other and take this one day at a time."

A Test of Trust

Around the house, moving boxes were half packed. A tearful Kylie was upstairs in her room, petting Whiskers and telling her how much she would miss her. Woof sat on the floor in the kitchen, listening to Mrs. Berryhill making phone calls to friends and animal shelters, looking for new homes for him and his animal buddies.

Ten minutes earlier, Mrs. Berryhill had put Billy down for a nap. On every other day, the toddler had napped quietly for at least an hour. But on this day, he climbed out of his crib and wandered into the living room.

Harriet was the first to see him. Right away, she knew something wasn't right. She squeaked out a warning to Presley, but the parrot was dozing and didn't hear her. She squeaked out to Wiggles, too, but he was nibbling at the stones on the bottom of his tank and did not notice her. Hoping to get someone's attention, Harriet started running on her wheel, which needed oiling and squeaked very loudly.

Meanwhile, the toddler was headed for the back door.

Finally, the parrot was roused by the hamster's squeaking wheel.

"Presley!" cried Harriet. "Do something! The kid is heading out the back door!"

Presley—who had an extremely loud voice—squawked for the cat, who heard him all the way from Kylie's room and streaked down the stairs in seconds.

"What's the matter?" Whiskers asked the squawking parrot.

"Follow the toddler!" the parrot cried. "No dawdling!"

Whiskers raced from the room and caught sight of the toddler just as he was wandering out the back door. Knowing she was powerless to stop him, she ran to find her friend Woof.

The dog was sniffing around some trash cans down the road.

"Woof, come quickly!" called the cat. "The toddler is heading for the swimming pool!"

Woof raced to the backyard and arrived just as the toddler was approaching the pool. He barked like there was no tomorrow and even lunged at the child to keep him from the water's edge.

Where on earth were the humans?

Inside, Mrs. Berryhill was finishing up her phone call with the Humane Society.

"They're pretty good pets," she said. "Yes, they're house trained. No, no diseases. Noisy? Well, not too much—"

But the shrill screeching of the parrot and the ferocious barking of the dog belied her.

"Listen, I have to go now," said Mrs. Berryhill. "I'll call back."

Just then Mr. Berryhill came charging down the stairs.

"What on earth is all that racket?" he yelled.

Kylie was right behind him. "What's going on?" she cried.

Together they ran into the backyard. Mr. Berryhill got there first and screamed at the dog.

"Quiet! You're disturbing the neighbors!"

But Woof kept up his barking. That's when everyone saw that the dog's barking and lunging at their toddler was the only thing keeping him out of the pool.

Mrs. Berryhill ran to the pool's edge and swept her little one into her arms.

With a look of intense relief, Mr. Berryhill embraced his wife and child.

"Thank goodness we got here in time," he said.

"Thank goodness the parrot started squawking and the dog started barking," said Mrs. Berryhill, tears of relief standing in her eyes.

Mr. Berryhill and Kylie turned to the dog.

"Good boy!" they said, leaning down and patting Woof's shoulders. "Good, good boy!"

Moving On

With her arms around Woof's neck and Whiskers rubbing her ankles, Kylie looked up at her parents.

"*Now* can we keep the animals?" she asked. "You promised!"

Mrs. Berryhill turned to her husband. "Kylie's right. We made the point that we had to be able to depend on these animals," she said. "Based on what just happened, I think they've proven they are **Dependable**."

Mr. Berryhill, who held his toddler snugly in his arms, nodded.

"You're right," he said. Mr. Berryhill kneeled down to look his daughter in the eye.

"Kylie, I gave you my word that if we could depend on the cat and dog to stop fighting, the animals could stay. I want you to be able to trust what I say. The way the animals have behaved today certainly earned my trust. I think we can figure out a way to take them with us."

"All of them?" Kylie asked pleadingly.

Mr. and Mrs. Berryhill looked at each other and smiled.

"Sure, why not?" said Mr. Berryhill with a laugh. "Let's do it."

And so it came to pass that Mr. Berryhill, Mrs. Berryhill, Kylie, Billy, the dog, the cat, the parrot, the hamster, and the goldfish piled into an RV and traveled together to their new home in a city on the other side of the country, where trust reigned supreme and they lived—more or less— happily ever after.

THE END

How Trustworthy Do You Think You Are?

Scoring Your Self-Assessment

As you read the parable, you had the opportunity to assess yourself in the areas of *Able, Believable, Connected,* and *Dependable.* We've reprinted the complete assessment on the following pages. It might be interesting for you to take it again—thinking about the same role you focused on earlier—to see if you've changed any of your answers. Or you can focus on another role in your life. For example, if you evaluated yourself in your role at work, now might be the time to evaluate yourself in your role at home. After you've filled out the assessment again, follow the directions on page 50 to find out how you scored.

Once again, here are the possible responses. On the following pages, circle the letter that best applies.

H—Hardly ever
S—Sometimes
O—Often
V—Very often
A—Always

ABLE
DEMONSTRATE COMPETENCE AND SKILLS

1. Get quality results   H S O V A
2. Solve problems   H S O V A
3. Am highly skilled   H S O V A
4. Am good at what I do   H S O V A
5. Have relevant experience   H S O V A
6. Use my skills to assist others   H S O V A
7. Strive to be the best at what I do   H S O V A

BELIEVABLE
ACT WITH INTEGRITY

8. Keep confidences   H S O V A
9. Admit when I am wrong   H S O V A
10. Am honest   H S O V A
11. Avoid talking behind people's backs   H S O V A
12. Am sincere   H S O V A
13. Am nonjudgmental   H S O V A
14. Show respect for others   H S O V A

CONNECTED
CARE ABOUT OTHERS

15. Listen well   H S O V A
16. Praise others' efforts   H S O V A
17. Show interest in others   H S O V A
18. Share about myself   H S O V A
19. Work well with others   H S O V A
20. Show empathy for others   H S O V A
21. Ask for input   H S O V A

DEPENDABLE
MAINTAIN RELIABILITY

22. Do what I say I will do   H S O V A
23. Am timely   H S O V A
24. Am responsive to requests   H S O V A
25. Am organized   H S O V A
26. Am accountable for my actions H S O V A
27. Follow up   H S O V A
28. Am consistent   H S O V A

ASSESSMENT TALLY

DIRECTIONS:

1. Enter the number of H, S, O, V, and A responses from the assessment for each section—A, B, C, and D.

2. Multiply by the number indicated and enter your result.

3. Add the results of each box to determine your total score for each section.

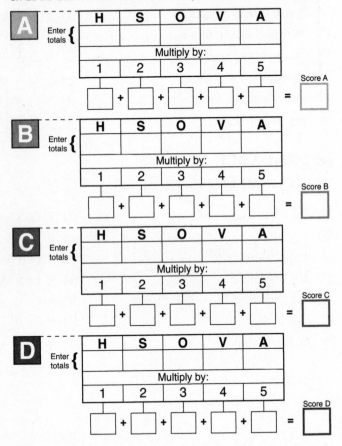

The following scoring legend will give you an idea how strong you are in each element of the ABCD Trust Model™.

> **33–35 = Outstanding! You've mastered this area.**
>
> **30–32 = Good. You're on the right track.**
>
> **27–29 = Average. Keep working at it.**
>
> **Below 27 = Pay attention! There's lots of room for improvement here.**

Questions to Ponder

Take a look at your scores and ponder the following questions:

1. In which element(s)—A (*Able*), B (*Believable*), C (*Connected*), or D (*Dependable*)—did you score highest?
2. In which element(s) did you score the lowest?
3. Did your results surprise you?

Part II

Trust-Building Resources

Applying the ABCD Trust Model™ to Real Life

Trust Busters and Trust Boosters

Understanding How Behaviors Affect Trust

When you understand how your behaviors affect others, it's much easier to gain respect, earn trust, and accomplish mutual goals.

Keep in mind that people usually won't come right out and tell you they don't trust you. Often the only indication you might have will be revealed by how a person acts around you. At work, for example, someone might withhold information from you, leave you out of meetings, walk the other way when they see you coming, or avoid eye contact. Assuming you would like to build a more trusting relationship with this person, where do you begin?

The first step is to recognize which behaviors build trust and which ones have the opposite effect. We call behaviors that encourage, build, and sustain trust Trust Boosters. Behaviors that undermine, damage, or destroy trust are Trust Busters.

In the following pages you'll find an extensive list of behaviors that either bust or boost trust. There's a lot of information here, so focus on the area where your score was lowest. If your lowest score was *Able,* go directly to page 58 and study the Trust Busters that are causing you trouble in this area—and the Trust Boosters that will help you become more trustworthy. If your lowest score was *Believable,* go to page 65. If your lowest score was *Connected*, go to page 72. And if your lowest score was *Dependable*, go to page 79.

Finally, don't just read the words on the page—make a commitment to put what you learn into practice. Once you've read up on eliminating Trust Busters and applying Trust Boosters in your weak area, go directly to page 86, where you'll learn how to check your self-perception by inviting others to assess you.

The ABCD Trust Model™

Able *Demonstrate Competence*	**Believable** *Act with Integrity*
• Get quality results	• Keep confidences
• Resolve problems	• Admit when you're wrong
• Develop skills	• Be honest
• Be good at what you do	• Don't talk behind backs
• Get experience	• Be sincere
• Use skills to assist others	• Be nonjudgmental
• Be the best at what you do	• Show respect
Connected *Care about Others*	**Dependable** *Maintain Reliability*
• Listen well	• Do what you say you'll do
• Praise others	• Be timely
• Show interest in others	• Be responsive
• Share about yourself	• Be organized
• Work well with others	• Be accountable
• Show empathy for others	• Follow up
• Ask for input	• Be consistent

Able

Behaviors That Bust and Boost Trust

**ABLE
Trust Buster #1:
Producing poor
or no results.**

Everyone has a bad day now and then, when their results are not what they or others expected of them. It's when the exception becomes the rule and shoddy or no work becomes your norm that people lose trust in your ability. If you become associated with a pattern of sloppy work, inaccurate data, incomplete assignments, and missed deadlines, you're not going to enjoy the benefits of being someone people trust.

**Trust Booster
Solution:
Work to get
quality results.**

If you want others to trust in your ability to handle a job, you need to demonstrate that you can do the work and do it well. When people see you producing consistent, quality results, they can relax in the knowledge that they have a strong team player—you—that they can trust to get the job done.

**ABLE
Trust Buster #2:
Failing to solve
problems.**

It may be tempting to
throw up your hands in
surrender at every obstacle,
but it's not going to inspire
people to trust in your
abilities. Problem solving
is as much about attitude
as it is about behavior. An
unwillingness to pitch in
and help is often at the root
of failing to solve problems.
If people come to expect
this from you, they'll turn
to someone else—because
you're not able and willing.

**Trust Booster
Solution:
Work to resolve
problems.**

To a great degree, life is
a series of problems to be
solved. This is as true in
one's personal life as it is
in one's work life. Rolling
up your sleeves and diving
in with the intention to
make a difference is often
half the battle in solving
problems. And there's
nothing wrong with asking
for help, provided your
intention is to get the
problem solved. By solving
problems you become a
person people see as able.

ABLE
Trust Buster #3:
Failing to develop skills.

Trust Booster
Solution:
Work to develop skills.

While it may be your heart's desire to be a trusted partner or team player, good intentions alone will not result in people having confidence in your ability. Just because someone has a passion to heal does not mean they're qualified to perform brain surgery. If you fail to invest the time and effort you need to develop skills, people can't rely on your ability.

It's often the case that problems require skills to be solved. When you are able to provide those skills, you increase your value as a trustworthy partner or team player. Whether you're an accountant, a zookeeper, or anything in between, bringing well-honed skills to the task at hand will not only solve problems, it will also engender trust in your ability.

ABLE
Trust Buster #4:
Being sloppy or
inconsistent
at what you do.

Some people spend their whole lives skating by, phoning it in, taking half measures, and settling for passing grades. That's their prerogative. But unless you're good at what you do, people won't trust in your ability. Plus, you won't enjoy the satisfaction of a job well done.

Trust Booster
Solution:
Work to become
good at
what you do.

Once you've selected your areas of expertise, give it all you've got to become a master. People who give a job their all frequently experience the joy of getting lost in their work. When others see this passion—and the subsequent excellent results—they trust your ability. Very often this leads to people singing your praises to others.

ABLE
Trust Buster #5:
Lacking relevant experience.

Most of us have encountered situations where we counted on someone to help us solve a problem and were let down, because the person didn't have the necessary experience to get the job done right. Not only does this waste time and energy, it also undermines trust. A good way to bust trust is to imply that you can get a job done when you don't have the experience to handle it.

Trust Booster
Solution:
Work to get relevant experience.

Knowledge and skills are essential to have, but they're only part of the story. To become a master, you also must have experience in your field. Just because you're a novice doesn't mean you're untrustworthy, but you will need to get some real-world experience before people can really rely on your ability in that area. Think of the comfort you feel when an experienced professional steps in to help you solve your problems. Don't you want others to view you with that same sense of security and trust?

**ABLE
Trust Buster #6:
Failing to assist
others.**

You might be the most
talented, experienced,
skilled woman in the
world or the smartest guy
in the room, but unless
you share your gifts with
others, you're not going to
win people's trust. Prima
donnas might get a lot of
attention, but they don't
win hearts and minds—let
alone trust.

**Trust Booster
Solution:
Use your skills
to assist others.**

Be generous with your
knowledge and skills. When
you extend your gifts to
others, you let them know
that you care—and that
builds trust.

ABLE
Trust Buster #7:
Not making an effort to
succeed at what you do.

Treading water might keep you from drowning, but it's not going to get you to the other side of the lake. When you don't make an effort to succeed at any given task or goal, it's bound to show. If you want people to trust in your ability, you need to put some energy into goal accomplishment.

Trust Booster
Solution:
Strive to be the best at
what you do.

Using your skills, producing quality work, and putting in your best effort to reach mutually agreed upon goals at work and at home will win the trust of others in your life.

Believable

Behaviors That Bust and Boost Trust

**BELIEVABLE
Trust Buster #1:
Violating confidences.**

It is an honor to be entrusted with sensitive information. Saying that you will keep a confidence and then leaking that information to others violates a sacred trust. If you can't be trusted to keep a confidence, your believability will plummet.

**Trust Booster
Solution:
Keep confidences.**

When someone tells you something in confidence, that means you don't repeat it—even to those you feel are "safe" to tell. When you have the integrity and maturity to keep a confidence, you make it safe for others to express sensitive information—and that increases your credibility.

BELIEVABLE
Trust Buster #2:
Refusing to admit
when you're wrong.

As we've said, everybody makes mistakes. When someone is too prideful to admit a mistake, it calls his or her judgment into question. People wonder, "What other blind spots does this person have?" Keeping quiet about your mistakes may protect your pride, but it won't make you believable or trustworthy.

Trust Booster
Solution:
Admit when you
are wrong.

Everybody makes mistakes, so it's inevitable that at some point you will be wrong about something. When you have the humility to recognize and admit that you are wrong, others come to have faith in your judgment—and that builds trust.

BELIEVABLE
Trust Buster #3:
Lying.

No one wants to think of themselves as a liar—but at one time or another, most of us are. Keep in mind that you don't have to tell an out-and-out whopper to undermine someone's trust. Those little white lies you rationalize about, when discovered, weaken relationships. So do lies of omission. When we leave out important information, we may not be verbalizing an actual lie, but we're misleading all the same. Less than forthright communication is one of the fastest ways to erode trust. Avoid it at all costs.

Trust Booster
Solution:
Be honest.

Across time and cultures, telling the truth has been a hallmark of trustworthy behavior. Expressions like "keep your word" or "you're only as good as your word" reveal that telling the truth is an essential component of integrity and key to building trust. Honesty includes forthrightness— not holding back when candor is warranted. This shows others that you are willing to risk repercussions if the situation requires directness—and makes you someone people can believe in.

BELIEVABLE
Trust Buster #4:
Talking behind
others' backs.

Want to ruin a relationship with someone? Say something less than complimentary about them behind their back. Sure, it's okay to sing someone's praises to others. Just make sure there's no "but" in your conversation. Even if you don't mean to say something harmful, just knowing that you're talking to others about them can raise a person's hackles. A great rule of thumb is to never say anything behind someone's back that you wouldn't say straight to the person's face. Be careful about listening to gossip, too. The person who's willing to talk behind the back of your acquaintance, coworker, or friend is probably quite comfortable gossiping about *you* when you're not around.

Trust Booster
Solution:
Avoid talking behind
people's backs.

We live in a gossipy culture. You can't go to the supermarket without seeing tabloids "talking" behind celebrities' backs. When you show others that you don't participate in this destructive behavior, they understand—at least intuitively—that you can probably be trusted not to talk about them behind their backs. Refusing to gossip is a rare habit worth cultivating, one that makes people feel safe around you.

**BELIEVABLE
Trust Buster #5:
Being insincere.**

We've all encountered them: people who lay on the charm and flattery, but whose underlying motives are self-centered. Sooner or later people can sift what's real from what's not. The person who makes a habit of making insincere statements soon gains a reputation for being a phony—and no one really trusts a phony.

**Trust Booster
Solution:
Be sincere.**

Sincerity is a matter of the heart. When you make a promise and keep it, when you give a compliment and mean it, when you smile with your eyes and not just your lips, people feel your sincerity and come to trust you. Always be sure that the words coming out of your mouth match the feelings in your heart.

**BELIEVABLE
Trust Buster #6:
Being judgmental.**

**Trust Booster
Solution:
Be nonjudgmental.**

There's a difference between discernment and judgment. Discernment is a powerful tool that can help us navigate life. Judgment, on the other hand, is a waste of time and energy that undermines trust. When we discern, we recognize differences in an impartial way. When we judge, our thoughts and words have an emotional charge that can be hurtful. When people feel judged, they stop trusting.

Humans are born with the inclination to distinguish good from bad, right from wrong, tasteful from tacky, beautiful from ugly—and on and on and on. We're hardwired to differentiate, and indeed this ability is one of the reasons we've survived and thrived as a species. Yet a person who can take it all in without passing judgment creates an atmosphere of safety that leads to trust. When you're nonjudgmental, people don't have to worry that you will judge *them*.

**BELIEVABLE
Trust Buster #7:
Disrespecting others.**

Knowledge can be a
dangerous thing. When
you think you know more
than anybody else, you're
in danger of committing
this trust buster. Every
time you belittle someone's
suggestion, disregard their
idea, or half listen to their
conversation, you are
draining the funds from
your trust account.

**Trust Booster
Solution:
Show respect for others.**

To build trust it is
essential to recognize that
everyone—regardless of
race, religion, education,
income, social status,
or any other variable—
is worthy of respect.
Extending respect to others
without prejudice gives
people confidence that
you are fair and therefore
trustworthy.

Connected

Behaviors That Bust and Boost Trust

CONNECTED
Trust Buster #1:
Poor listening.

Do you listen with the intent to be moved or informed—or do you merely tolerate others' conversation, waiting for the opportunity to jump in with your own agenda? If you can't absorb what others are saying, you can't connect with them—and they can't connect with you. People have a hard time trusting those who don't get them.

Trust Booster
Solution:
Listen well.

Listening is more than waiting for the other person to stop talking. When you listen well— reflecting back what you see and hear—you build a bridge to understanding and trust.

**CONNECTED
Trust Buster #2:
Ignoring others'
efforts.**

It's hard to feel secure
when there's a vacuum
of information. If people
have put forth energy in
your direction—at work,
at home, even in a casual
business transaction—
and all they hear back is a
deafening silence, you're
busting their trust. Yes,
sometimes it takes time
and effort to give tactful,
candid feedback—but
when you don't, you're not
building trust.

**Trust Booster
Solution:
Praise others'
efforts.**

Catch people doing things
right! When you recognize
others with praise, you let
them know that you're on
their side, rooting for them.
Sincere praise is one of the
most effective ways to build
trust. If it's appropriate,
make your praise public.
When you announce to
the world the specific,
fine qualities or work of
another, you create the
kind of bond that promotes
trust.

CONNECTED
Trust Buster #3:
Showing no interest in others.

We're all wrapped up in our own worlds, so it's easy to ignore each other. Bosses ignore employees. Employees ignore bosses. Husbands ignore wives. Wives ignore husbands. Friends ignore friends. While we can't provide others with our undivided attention all the time, we can acknowledge them. It takes less time to say, "I hear you. I'll get back to you as soon as I can," than to repair the damage that ignoring can do to a relationship. Just as showing up is a way to build trust, showing no interest in others is a sure way to lose it.

Trust Booster
Solution:
Show interest in others.

Recognizing that you are not the center of the universe and showing interest in others opens up the doors to trust. By zeroing in on the world outside your own head— observing others' concerns and feelings—you become more aware of what is required to create a trusting environment.

CONNECTED
Trust Buster #4: Failing to share about yourself.

Perhaps you're a person who feels safer holding back—or holding tightly to ideas, things, and feelings like love. Just as sunlight cannot pour through a window with the curtains closed, trust cannot enter your life if you hide behind a wall. Ironically, this trust-busting behavior is the result of your own lack of trust and a fear that there's not enough to go around. Not only does failing to share about yourself undermine trust, it's also contagious. When people see you withholding, they often start withholding as well, out of defensiveness.

Trust Booster
Solution: Share about yourself.

When you open up and share about yourself, you demonstrate a vulnerability that engenders trust. Others feel more at ease when they can relate to you. By sharing about your hobbies, travels, or other interests, people feel they know you a little better. You should never reveal highly personal or private information unless you choose to do so.

**CONNECTED
Trust Buster #5:
Working poorly
with others.**

Criticizing others' work, dismissing others' ideas, failing to show appreciation for others' efforts, and excluding others from decision making are great ways to disconnect from the people you work with. They're also terrific ways to create a distrustful, toxic work environment.

**Trust Booster
Solution:
Work well
with others.**

Validate the people you work with. When you corroborate others' ideas and show appreciation for their efforts, you not only build trust, you also create the kind of rock-solid support that will help you and others soar. Include the input of others as you make decisions. By doing so, you demonstrate trust in them—and that leads to others trusting in you.

CONNECTED
Trust Buster #6:
Being insensitive to others.

It's a sad fact that we can hurt one another in countless ways: physical blows, emotional punches, financial deprivation, mental harassment—the list could go on. Especially when you are feeling hurt or weak yourself, take care not to project that pain onto someone else by behaving in a hurtful way. The first thing that will be damaged will be the trust between you and the person you hurt.

Trust Booster Solution:
Show empathy for others.

Being sensitive to others' feelings opens the door to trust. Even when you have to deliver less-than-good news, by treating people as you would wish to be treated, you will earn their trust. Empathy also includes encouragement. Everybody needs a cheerleader. By giving strength and encouragement to others, you become a member of their trusted support team.

**CONNECTED
Trust Buster #7:
Failing to ask for input.**

Whether it's because you think you have all the answers or because you're afraid to solicit ideas, failing to ask for input leaves you isolated from others. Not a great way to connect and build trust.

**Trust Booster
Solution:
Ask for input.**

No one of us is as smart as all of us. When you open up and solicit others' good ideas, you not only build trust, you also get smarter. Seek opinions from a variety of sources, paying particular attention to those with whom you might not ordinarily agree. The broader your base, the more connected you'll be.

Dependable

Behaviors That Bust and Boost Trust

**DEPENDABLE
Trust Buster #1:
Failing to do what
you say you will do.**

People break commitments so frequently that many don't even realize they're violating a trust when they do it: the manager who cancels a meeting at the last minute because "something came up"; the woman who cancels dinner with a friend on short notice because she got a better offer; the direct report who fails to turn in a promised project. Just because they're common doesn't mean these behaviors don't undermine trust. If you have made a commitment—spoken or implied—you need to follow through or at least explain why you cannot.

**Trust Booster
Solution:
Do what you say
you will do.**

Your word is your commitment. There's a difference between interest and commitment. When you're interested, you may or may not follow through. When you're committed, you do it. For example, a person interested in exercise skips his daily walk when it's raining outside. The person who's committed to exercise works out at the gym that day. When you show up as someone who follows through on your stated commitments, you become a person people can depend on.

**DEPENDABLE
Trust Buster #2:
Being late.**

Good intentions are no substitute for being on time. When you show up late to meetings, you disrespect others' time. When you miss a deadline without providing forewarning or explanation, you again disrespect others—and that violates their trust.

**Trust Booster
Solution:
Be timely.**

Showing up on time and producing results when you say you will are two of the best ways to show people you are trustworthy. Because time is limited, meeting deadlines can sometimes be a struggle. Making the effort to be timely communicates to others that you care—a real trust builder.

**DEPENDABLE
Trust Buster #3:
Not responding
to requests.**

Everyone, it seems, is busy today. E-mail in-boxes and voice mails are overflowing with messages, calendars are full, and days feel too short to get it all done. So it's easy to rationalize why you can't respond to requests. Yet if you wish to inspire trust in your dependability, you must.

**Trust Booster
Solution:
Be responsive to
requests.**

To greet a request with an attitude of cheerful service is to build a bridge to trust. Note that responding to a request does not mean fulfilling a request—that will depend on your available time and energy. A pleasant response takes only a moment, but it shows you are dependable and pays off big dividends in trust.

DEPENDABLE
Trust Buster #4:
Being
disorganized.

Lost files, lost e-mails,
missed messages, missed
meetings—add them all
up and they produce an
unreliable human being.
Even if being organized
is not your strong suit,
you will have to develop
some skill in this area for
people to count on you as
dependable.

Trust Booster
Solution:
Work to become
organized.

Creating order puts
you and others at ease.
Establishing systems and
processes and developing
project plans make work
simpler and life more
manageable. If you don't
have these skills, find
someone to set up systems
that work for you and to
coach you about how to
maintain them. When you
live an organized life, you
help yourself and others
accomplish goals—which in
turn creates trust.

**DEPENDABLE
Trust Buster #5:
Failing to be
accountable for
your actions.**

Perhaps you're a fiercely independent person who balks at the idea of having to account to anybody for your actions. You know why you do what you do, and that's good enough for you. Fine. But if you desire to be someone people can trust and rely on, you're going to have to check in and discuss your hits and misses with others.

**Trust Booster
Solution:
Be accountable
for your
actions.**

It's often said that no man is an island. Because we're interconnected, your actions—good or bad—have an effect on others. When you own up to your actions and take responsibility for them, others begin to see you as someone they can count on.

**DEPENDABLE
Trust Buster #6:
Not following up.**

Failing to follow through on one's responsibilities has long been a characteristic of the typical trust buster. It's often what comes to mind when people hear the word "untrustworthy." People can't trust you if they can't count on you to follow up. If you avoid all the other Trust Busters and yet fail to honor your obligations, people are still not going to trust you.

**Trust Booster
Solution:
Follow up.**

When you set a goal or make an agreement, follow up. Even if you haven't yet completed your agreed-upon goals, follow up by showing up and saying so. Woody Allen famously said, "Eighty percent of success is simply showing up." When you follow up, you complete the other 20 percent—and people trust you as dependable.

DEPENDABLE
Trust Buster #7:
Being inconsistent.

Okay, you didn't mean to
lie or deceive—you just had
a sudden change of plans.
It happens to the best of
us. As psychologists know,
intermittent reinforcement
drives people crazy. The
extent to which there's an
inconsistency between our
actions and our behaviors is
the degree to which other
people will or won't trust
us. The winning formula is
simple: Walk your talk.

Trust Booster
Solution:
Behave consistently.

Sometimes predictability
is a good thing. When you
speak and behave with
consistency, rather than
letting your moods dictate
your behavior, people come
to know you as someone
they can depend on—and
that builds trust.

This is just a partial list. As you continue on your
journey to becoming a master of trust, you will
undoubtedly discover other Trust Busters and
Boosters. Remember that like anything in life,
practice makes perfect. You may not transform
your Trust Busters into Trust Boosters overnight,
but with awareness and action you'll make steady
progress.

Checking Your Self-Perception

Invite Others to Assess You

Because trust is a two-way street, your self-assessment is only part of the picture of your overall trustworthiness. That's why we have included another ABCD assessment at the back of the book. (See the appendix on page 127, "How Trustworthy Do You Think I Am?" The assessment is also available online at www.trustworksbook.com.) We suggest you make copies of this assessment and ask people in your workplace, at home, or in other social networks to rate you in the areas of *Able, Believable, Connected,* and *Dependable.* Then compare your self-assessment with the assessments of those who know you well.

It is important to set up the process correctly, so people will be candid in their assessments and won't fear retaliation for their answers. Encourage them to leave their names off the assessment, unless they choose to be identified with their feedback. Explain that their responses will help you become more aware of how your behavior is perceived by others.

Once you have all the assessments, compile the responses and put the totals into the summary score sheet on page 130. Next, identify your strong trust areas as well as areas where you have room for improvement. Now compare these to your own assessment. See where you have similarities and where you have differences. Decide what you want to start, stop, and continue as trust behaviors. Using the Trust Boosters in the previous section to guide you, create an action plan. Remember to thank everyone for their responses and tell them what you have learned about yourself.

Ken did this with his team at work. The results showed considerable agreement between his perception and theirs. His highest score was *Connected* and his lowest was *Dependable*. When he and his team looked at why everyone felt that *Dependable* was his weak area, they determined it was because Ken never really heard a bad idea—in other words, he said yes too easily. As a result, he often became overcommitted, and that put stress on both him and his team.

To help Ken become more **Dependable,** the group talked with him about various strategies. Margery Allen, his executive assistant, suggested that when Ken went on business trips he should pass out her business card instead of his, so she could help screen callers and talk with Ken about which business proposals were realistic considering his time, energy, and the team's resources. That strategy has been highly successful in making Ken more **Dependable**.

Now that you have a sense of your strong and weak trust areas, we'll show you how to diagnose trust issues and use the ABCD Trust Model™ to resolve breakdowns in trust.

Learning to Diagnose Trust Issues

How to Recognize Trust Busters

Your self-assessment and the assessments of others have given you a good idea about where your strengths and weaknesses are. You've looked at which Trust Busters might be undermining your ability to build and sustain trust. As you read the Trust Busters that applied to you, perhaps you had the same reaction Ken did: "How do they know me so well?" You've also reviewed the corresponding Trust Boosters that can help you get back on track.

The next step is to learn how to diagnose low-trust situations to find out what behavior or behaviors are causing the breakdown in trust. Generally, behaviors will fall within one or more elements of the ABCD Trust Model™—*Able, Believable, Connected,* or *Dependable*.

Let's review a couple of easy scenarios from the story to get a very basic idea of how diagnosis works.

Diagnosing Trust Issues
Scenario 1: Mr. B's Dilemma

In "Broken Trust," Mrs. Berryhill comments to her husband that his reaction to the broken dishes (threatening to get rid of all the pets) seemed out of proportion to the incident. She asks him if something was bothering him. Mr. Berryhill acknowledged that work was bothering him. His boss had made the comment that he was disappointed Mr. Berryhill didn't seem to have the skills to get his job done on his own.

From the point of view of Mr. Berryhill's boss, which element of the ABCD Trust Model™— *Able, Believable, Connected,* or *Dependable*— was causing him to lose trust in Mr. Berryhill? In other words, which element best describes the behaviors Mr. Berryhill was exhibiting that were causing a breakdown in trust?

*The answer is A. Mr. Berryhill's boss did not feel he was **Able** to do the job. He was not getting the desired results due to his lack of skills in this area of his job.*

Diagnosing Trust Issues
Scenario 2: The Cat's Dilemma

In the story, Woof makes many efforts to win Whiskers's trust. Finally, he wins her over. But when the cat feels everything is fine between them, she's dismayed to hear that the dog does not yet trust *her*. She comments to the others, "I've proclaimed my friendship. How am I supposed to make this dumb dog see the truth?"

Which element of the ABCD Trust Model™ was lacking in the cat's behavior?

*The answer is C. The cat's lack of empathy for the dog's point of view reveals that she had a problem being **Connected**.*

In real life, of course, elements of the ABCD Trust Model™ are not always so easy to diagnose, and the answers are not always so cut-and-dried. In the next section we'll examine how people's different perceptions about trustworthy behavior affect relationships, and how you can converse in a common language to overcome these barriers to trust.

Learning to Have Trust Conversations

The Importance of Perception

Trust means different things to different people, because we all see the world differently. This is why we often say, "Trust is in the eyes of the beholder." It's a matter of perception, just as in the well-known story of five blind men all describing the same elephant: the one who feels the leg says it's like a tree; the one who feels the tail swears it's like a rope; the one who feels the elephant's trunk is sure it's like a snake; the one who feels its ear insists it's like a fan; the one who feels its side is sure the elephant is like a wall. In the same way, people see behaviors from their own points of view.

The elephant analogy illustrates the importance of making certain we look at trust issues from others' points of view. To build our understanding of each other and get a sense of the big picture, we need to view life from perspectives other than our own.

With differing perceptions in mind, let's move on to some more challenging scenarios and see how we can use the ABCD Trust Model™ to begin trust-building conversations.

Practicing Trust Conversations
Scenario 1: You and Your Son

Suppose you are the father of a teenage son named Will. The two of you never seem to see eye to eye on any topic or issue. You want to build a better relationship with your son, and he says he'd like an easier relationship with you.

Seeing an opening here, you show your son the ABCD Trust Model™ and talk about Trust Boosters and Trust Busters. You might ask him to think about the things his good friends do to boost trust and the things other kids might have done that busted his trust. You suggest that the two of you could use the model to diagnose the trust elements that are lacking in your interactions and to build a closer relationship. Will says he's open to trying it so that life can be easier between the two of you.

To ensure Will has time to study, you have established a rule that he cannot go out during the school week. Furthermore, he is not allowed to watch television, surf the Internet, or use his cell phone until all his homework is done. Additionally, he has to be home on the weekends by 12:00 midnight. In spite of this, Will frequently misses his curfew. He does not call home to say where he is or that he is going to be late. You sit up waiting for him to come home, no matter what the hour.

One night Will comes home at two in the morning. You meet him in the front hall and ask why he is home way past his curfew. He says his friend's car broke down. "Plus," he says, "the car ran out of gas and we were out of range for cell-phone coverage, so I couldn't call." You later find out this isn't true.

Using the ABCD Trust Model™ to Start the Conversation

It might be tempting for you to give Will a lecture and sentence him to some form of punishment. While making Will face consequences for his behavior is appropriate, a lecture at this moment will do nothing to build the trust between you.

Start by expressing your sincere desire to build a more positive relationship. Then use the ABCD Trust Model™ as a tool to facilitate the discussion. For example, you might begin by saying:

"Will, we talked earlier about building a better relationship. I feel like the trust has broken down between us and I'd like to use this Trust Model to figure out what's not working and how we can fix it."

Next, address the issue and state your perception of what area of the model has been affected. For example:

"You've been home past our agreed-upon curfew several times lately, and you haven't called to explain. When you're late and don't do what you say you'll do, it makes me feel like I can't count on you to be *Dependable*."

At this point the conversation might go something like this:

"I told you, Dad, my friend's car broke down and we were out of cell-phone range."

"That's another thing," you might say. "I talked to your friend and found out that just isn't true. We'll talk about the consequences for that later. What's important to me now is our relationship. When you don't tell the truth, that's a real Trust Buster. It's hard to have a good relationship when I'm not sure you're *Believable*."

At this point your son might mumble an apology or another excuse. In either case, you want this to be a dialogue, not a lecture, so you continue:

"I know trust isn't a one-way street. Where on the model have I busted trust with you?"

Will studies the ABCD Trust Model™. To your surprise he says:

"To be honest, I don't feel like you're **Connected,** Dad. You always say you're proud of my athletic accomplishments, but you've only attended one of my track meets this year. And during the one meet you did attend, you sat in the bleachers using your cell phone while other parents were cheering like crazy for their kids. And even though I've won a bunch of medals, you don't ever brag about me to your friends."

Taken aback, you might say, "I'm sorry I busted your trust that way. The truth is, I'm extremely proud of you! I promise in the future I'll attend more meets and leave my cell phone in my pocket. And I thought bragging about you to my friends embarrassed you—it always did when you were a kid. I would love to brag about you!"

Because you want to reach a mutual understanding, you might now say:

"Can I count on you to be more *Dependable* about keeping your curfew and more *Believable* by telling the truth?"

At this point your son surprises you again.

"I'm not really done, Dad," he says. "I'm getting really good grades, but you're treating me like a little kid. Your strict rules about me not watching TV or using my phone or the Internet make me feel like you don't trust me. I feel like if you were really *Connected,* you'd understand that my grades are important to me, too. You'd give me credit for being *Able* and *Dependable* about my homework and you wouldn't be so controlling."

"Wow," you might say. "Thanks for telling me that. My intention was to support your academic achievements by helping you establish proven study habits. I can see now how you might feel I was out of touch."

The conversation, of course, could go any number of ways. The point is that the two of you, using the ABCD Trust Model™ as a guide, are talking, sharing your perceptions, and coming to agreements about building a more trusting relationship.

Practicing Trust Conversations
Scenario 2: Your Product Work Team

Let's move on to the workplace arena.

Suppose you are on a team that has been working on a state-of-the-art technology product to simplify the data entry systems within hospitals. Your team has eight members—representing different areas of expertise—who are working to create this new product. The eight of you have been together for a year and a half.

Unfortunately, your team has failed to meet several of its deadlines, including one that was critical. You and your team members did not explain to your leadership why the delay occurred, nor did you offer any plans to rectify the situation.

Your team was proactive, however, when one of your team members attempted to use a competitor's data without permission. The rest of you stepped in and stopped him, saying that his behavior was not ethical. You and your team members explained that because you did not want the team to get a bad reputation, you would not accept this behavior.

Furthermore, your team had to work through some difficult production challenges. Due to its collective knowledge of hospital data entry systems and its skills in product development, your team was able to overcome the obstacles and produce a working prototype.

In spite of your team's successful work output, some of the team members often found reason to talk about the others behind their backs. On top of that, members rarely praised or acknowledged each other's work.

Talking About Perceptions to Build Trust on a Team

While managing the team is the role of the team leader, many teams have no team leader, or the designated leader is failing to lead. Regardless of your official title, you can fill the leadership void by requesting to be on the agenda and speaking at your next team meeting.

Begin the conversation by recapping the team's shared goals. Using the ABCD Trust Model™ as a framework for discussion, you might continue the discussion by saying:

"Let's take a moment to assess how we're doing as a team in these four areas. There are a lot of things we're doing right. For example, when we confronted you, Bob, about your poor decision to use a competitor's data without permission, we were being honest and showing respect for others' work. So I think our behavior made us *Believable* on that one.

"Another positive," you might continue, "was producing that prototype. Because we had relevant expertise and effective skills, we were *Able* to perform well. We make a regular practice of Trust Boosters like getting quality results and using our collective experience to solve problems. Before I go any further, what do the rest of you feel proud of that we're doing as a team?"

At this point, hear and acknowledge others' input. Then move the discussion toward diagnosing Trust Busters.

"Now let's look at where we could be more successful. Let's again use the ABCD Trust Model™ as a guide.

"From my perspective, we are not being successful as a team because we're not performing well. I'd like us to talk about that issue."

As you talk, remember to take responsibility for your own failings:

"Because our team—myself included—hasn't been accountable for our work output, we did not take responsibility when we missed a deadline. I feel our team failed to be *Dependable*. What do the rest of you think?"

Again referring to the ABCD Trust Model™, you could guide the team by saying:

"What Trust Boosters could we use to rebuild trust with our leadership in this area?" Here you and the team might suggest that you could do what you say you'll do, be accountable for your actions, and follow up in a timely way, keeping your leadership informed about the project. You might add:

"We're also falling short in the areas of being *Connected* and *Believable*. The way some of us ignore each other's efforts and talk behind each other's backs are real Trust Busters."

Keeping in mind that trust is a matter of perception, you might say:

"I've given you my point of view about these issues and I know it's just one way of looking at things. I'd like to hear more from you about how you feel and what you think we can do to build trust as a team and with our leadership."

However you choose to guide the conversation, taking the initiative to address these issues and putting them on the table for open discussion could do more to help your team and organization than your most brilliant individual contribution. Like the animals in the parable, a trusting team working together often makes the difference between breakthrough success and dismal failure.

Practicing Trust Conversations
Scenario 3: You and Your Spouse

While we don't claim to be marriage counselors, we do want to show how the ABCD Trust Model™ can be used to clarify different perceptions and build trust in a personal relationship. With that caveat in mind, consider the following.

Suppose you and your spouse have been married for eleven years. You are both career professionals and you have no children. Finding time to take a joint vacation has been challenging and has become a point of contention. Six times you have suggested calendar dates; each time your spouse has replied that those times did not work. You have commented to your spouse that you believe he does not want to spend time with you, otherwise he would be making a greater effort to take time off. Your spouse has dismissed your comments with responses like, "That's ridiculous."

Fortunately, your spouse gets the message. At dinner he presents you with several travel brochures, plane schedules, and potential itineraries he's acquired from your travel agent, as well as specific dates he's scheduled to take time off for your vacation.

You want to make certain your spouse's plans are for real, so you call his personal assistant to see if the time has been reserved on your spouse's calendar for the vacation and that reservations have been made with the travel agent.

Later, you tell your spouse that when he initially dismissed your attempts to find time to vacation together, your feelings were hurt. You also state that spending time together is very important to you. You thank and praise him for making the effort to join you on vacation.

Using the ABCD Trust Model™ to Clear Up Misperceptions

The vacation situation is one of many recurring incidents that cause friction in your marriage. Rather than just letting it go, you decide to use the ABCD Trust Model™ to open up a dialogue and see if you and your spouse can change this pattern.

You begin by affirming your intention to build a more trusting relationship. Next, using the model, you explain that when your spouse dismissed your sincere attempts to spend vacation time together—as well as your concern that he doesn't want to spend time with you—you felt he was not listening or empathizing with your feelings—in other words, based on his behavior, you did not feel he was *Connected*.

Your spouse, perhaps feeling a bit defensive, counters that he solved the problem by doing his homework and bringing information to plan the vacation, demonstrating that he was *Able*. He also felt he had been *Dependable*, because he did what he said he was going to do.

You thank him again for planning the vacation. You mention that you did praise him for that, making an attempt to stay *Connected*. You also mention that by mustering the courage to tell him the truth about your hurt feelings, you felt you were acting in a way that was *Believable*.

Your spouse says that he never intended to hurt your feelings. He then points out that he didn't feel very good when you called his assistant to check that he really had put the vacation on his calendar and the travel reservations really had been made. He says this felt like you were checking up on him and questioning his integrity. He didn't think your behavior was *Believable*, because he felt you were judging him as unreliable and didn't respect his word.

You apologize for having come off that way and explain that you had a completely different view of your actions. You thought you were being *Dependable* by being organized and following up to make certain the dates were on his calendar.

While the ABCD Trust Model™ alone can't solve all your marriage issues, it can provide you with a framework for discussing situations that may be causing discord. By using the model to look at each other's perceptions and clear up misunderstandings, you and your spouse can clear the air and build trust in your relationship.

Practicing Trust Conversations
Scenario 4: Your Sales Manager

Suppose you work in the sales division of a medium-sized wholesale company that has been hard hit by a weakened economy. One of your former colleagues, Susan—the niece of the company's owners—has been promoted to be your manager. While Susan parrots the company's stated value that honesty and integrity always come before profit and short-term gain, she ignores the fact that one of your team members, Joe, repeatedly accepts financial kickbacks from clients. In fact, because Joe is a high performer, she rewards him with generous bonuses.

As a new manager, Susan is having difficulty delegating. She still insists on attending every meeting in the department, requires overly detailed reports from each team member, focuses on procedural trivia, and makes decisions that team members are perfectly capable of making for themselves. Although she rarely assigns projects, when she does, she closely supervises every step, taking credit for successes and reprimanding for less-than-perfect results.

Susan's people skills leave something to be desired. Even though she smiles and makes small talk, when people converse with her, they get the sense she is only half listening, as she expresses no real interest in their concerns. She rarely, if ever, shares information about herself. When she is disappointed in the performance of a team member, she openly criticizes that person in team meetings, causing some embarrassing and even humiliating situations.

When Susan assumed the sales manager role, she announced that she was going to bring the department into the twenty-first century with new technology and expanded resources. Yet months later, no progress has been made toward these goals. Team members' written requests for updated technology are ignored. When team members ask directly about the much-needed resources, Susan deflects their questions by changing the subject.

Applying the ABCD Trust Model™ in Difficult Business Situations: Is the Conversation Worth the Risk?

Here we have a case—not unheard of in the real world—where a person with significant position power is busting trust in all four quadrants of the ABCD Trust Model™.

Because Susan's assertion that she upholds the company's values is not consistent with her looking the other way when Joe receives kickbacks, she is not *Believable*.

Because she lacks relevant experience, micromanages, and has failed to rise to the requirements of her new role, Susan has demonstrated that she does not have the skills of a leader and therefore is not *Able* to manage the team.

Because Susan is a poor listener, shows little interest in others, withholds information about herself, and criticizes people publicly, she shows that she is not *Connected*.

Finally, because she has not followed through on her commitment to upgrade the department's technology, ignores her team members' requests, and does not follow up, Susan has demonstrated that she is not *Dependable*.

It takes courage to begin a conversation about trust in almost every situation. But this case is particularly challenging, since Susan not only has position power but political power as well—she's the owners' niece. In cases like these, it's important to assess the risk of speaking out.

A wise person once said that sometimes when there's no warmth from a dying fire, it's silly to sit there and complain about the cold. Somebody has to throw the first log on the coals. If you have assessed the risk and decided it's better to speak out than to accept the status quo, a good way to begin is by modeling the behavior you wish to see in your boss. You might share the ABCD Trust Model™ with her and open a dialogue by asking her what behaviors she sees in you that boost and bust her trust. Give her the "How Trustworthy Do You Think I Am?" assessment in the back of this book and let her evaluate you. In time your relationship may develop to the point where you feel safe to reciprocate by gently bringing up some of her trust-busting behaviors.

Applying the ABCD Trust Model™ to Your Own Life

Where in *your* life is trust lacking?

Now that you've seen how to use the ABCD Trust Model™, think about a relationship in your own life where you feel you have not gained the trust of another or where you have low trust in someone else. Keeping this relationship in mind, answer the following questions:

- What Trust Buster behaviors have led to the strain in this relationship?
- What element of the ABCD Trust Model™ is being impacted by these behaviors?
- Assuming the relationship is important to you and you're willing to take the risk, how might you use ABCD Trust Model™ to begin a conversation and bridge the trust gap?

Remember that even though your perceptions are likely to be different from the person you have an issue with, the model will give you a framework to begin that all-important dialogue. Using the ABCDs, you can talk with the other person about where trust was busted and discuss which Trust Boosters could be applied to restore mutual understanding, empathy, and partnership.

Although the ABCD Trust Model™ is simple, applying the model to your own trust issues is not. With practice, however, using the model to start trust conversations gets easier. In the end, we're confident you'll find the benefits are well worth any initial discomfort.

But what if a situation in your life involves a serious violation of trust that has all but destroyed the relationship? In the next section, we'll outline a five-step process for rebuilding damaged trust.

Rebuilding Damaged Trust

Despite our best intentions, at one time or another all of us break trust with others. In fact, because people have different perceptions of trust, misunderstandings and relationship strains are fairly common. We've seen how having a conversation using the ABCD Trust Model™ as a guide can help in these circumstances. But what do you do when a breach of trust is so severe that the relationship is strained to the breaking point— or breaks completely?

We call this damaged trust.

If you are avoiding another person because you feel there is no safe way to communicate openly, you are probably experiencing damaged trust. If the very thought of approaching this person fills you with dread, anger, or fear, that's another sign that you're dealing with damaged trust.

Contending with damaged trust requires fortitude and forethought. A conversation with the party in question is likely to be challenging. Emotions will be volatile and the stakes will be high. Additionally, the conversation could have consequences you would rather avoid.

If you feel a situation is so explosive—or the stakes are so perilous—that a conversation could cause further damage, you probably need to engage the services of a qualified mediator or therapist. If, on the other hand, you have assessed the challenges and decided that the risks are manageable, you can follow this five-step process to begin rebuilding the relationship and restoring trust.

Step One: Acknowledge and Assure

To begin the rebuilding process, the first step is to acknowledge that a problem exists and needs to be addressed. If you are initiating the trust conversation, this will require courage. As you acknowledge the problem, assure the other party that your intention is to restore trust between the two of you and that you are willing to take the time and effort to get the relationship back on track. It is important to find out if your goal of rebuilding the relationship is mutual. If it is not, there is little you can do, other than thank them for their honesty. You may—or may not—want to let the person know that if they change their mind, you will be open to a conversation in the future.

Step Two: Admit

The next step is to admit your part in causing the breach of trust. Own up to your actions and take responsibility for whatever harm was caused. Even if you don't feel you are entirely at fault, admit to your part in the situation. In cases where you feel the other party is mostly to blame, your part might be as simple as "I admit I haven't let you know what's been bothering me." Admitting your part in the situation is a crucial step that should not be overlooked. Refusing to admit your mistakes undermines your believability.

Step Three: Apologize

The third step in repairing damaged trust is to apologize for your role in the situation. This takes humility. Again, even if you don't feel you were entirely at fault, apologize for your part in the situation. Express regret for any harm you may have caused and assure the other person you will change the undesirable behavior. ("I apologize for avoiding you. In the future I will let you know right away when I have a problem.") It's important that your apology is sincere and that you feel authentic remorse. If it's contrived or forced, the other person will pick up on that and question your believability. Avoid making excuses, shifting blame, or using qualifying statements, as these will undermine your apology.

Step Four: Assess

Invite feedback from the other party about how he or she sees the situation. Together, assess which elements of the ABCD Trust Model™ were violated. Discussing the behaviors that damaged the relationship is bound to bring up uncomfortable emotions, so be prepared. It will be helpful to affirm that the purpose of this step is not to point fingers, but rather to identify problem behaviors so they can be avoided in the future. The more specific you can be about the behaviors that damaged the trust, the easier it will be to repair the breach, as you'll each have a clear idea about what needs to change.

Step Five: Agree

The final step in rebuilding damaged trust is to work together to create an action plan. Now that you have discussed each other's perceptions and identified the specific Trust Busters at the root of the problem, you can mutually identify the Trust Boosters you'll use going forward. This is the time to clarify your shared goals for the relationship and make requests about what you'd both like to see more or less of in the future.

• • •

Building trust is important in all relationships, but it's particularly important if you hold a position of authority. If you're a leader, you can afford many kinds of mistakes, but the one thing you can't afford is to lose trust. By practicing behaviors that align with the four core elements of trust, you will not only set a healthy example, you will also inspire enthusiasm and success in those who follow you.

In the next section, we'll examine how leaders can create trust in their organizations.

Building Trust in Organizations
A Message for Leaders

The ability to build trust is the defining competency for leaders in the twenty-first century. Smart organizations are increasingly taking proactive steps to build high-trust cultures, because they've seen clear evidence that it helps improve the bottom line. With trust, creativity flourishes, productivity rises, barriers are overcome, and relationships deepen. Without it, people bail on relationships and leave organizations, cynicism reigns, progress grinds to a halt, and self-interest trumps the common good. For organizations to thrive, trust is not a nice-to-have; it's a must-have.

Most people don't give a lot of thought to intentionally building trust; they just assume it happens over time. Teaching people how to address trust issues in the workplace before they reach a crisis stage—and employees leave—is one of the most needed skills in today's work environment.

Organizational trust is built on everyday actions. Most of us have dealt with broken promises, unfulfilled commitments, leaders withholding information, unfair treatment, lies, and dishonesty, which are all too common in the workplace. Repeated occurrences of these trust-busting behaviors by leaders foster low-trust environments, resulting in employees who are demoralized, disengaged, unproductive, afraid to take risks, and ultimately at a higher risk to leave the organization.

Usually there is no safe way to discuss problems that have grown due to a lack of trust, such as poor morale, interdepartmental and interpersonal conflicts, poor customer service, and lack of communication. The beauty of the ABCD Trust Model™ is that it takes the complex subject of trust and simplifies it into a framework that leaders at all levels can use to build more trusting relationships.

A Board of Directors Breakthrough:
A Real-World Case Study

The transformation of the culturally diverse board of directors of a well-known corporation illustrates the power of the ABCD Trust Model™. The board members had abruptly walked out of their previous session due to major disagreements they were unable to resolve. Disparaging remarks and hurtful epithets had been exchanged, which not only created turmoil and hard feelings, but also wiped out any feelings of trust.

Cindy facilitated a reconciliation session with the twenty directors. The atmosphere was tense. As facilitator, Cindy addressed the purpose of the meeting, stating that the desired outcomes were to reach an understanding and determine the next steps to moving forward. She also stated that a lack of trust among them was at the heart of the problem.

To create a framework for discussion, Cindy introduced the group to the ABCD Trust Model™. She then divided the twenty directors into four tables. Each table was assigned one of the four trust elements: *Able, Believable, Connected,* and *Dependable.* She asked each group to create a list of behaviors within that element that they wanted their board of directors to use to reestablish trust and build a more harmonious working environment. She gave them forty-five minutes to complete the exercise.

The *Able* team presented first. Their spokesperson shared their recommendations for being capable and competent as a team, offering ideas about sharing knowledge and expertise, applying past experience from being on other corporate boards, knowing the key issues, practicing good governance, being prepared by understanding items in the board packet, and asking relevant questions.

The *Believable* team went next. Their spokesperson, Monique—dressed in traditional African attire and head scarf—rose and spoke in a quiet but powerful voice:

"Our table feels strongly that we need to value each other's cultural differences, hold ourselves accountable to our core values, be open and honest, plus speak and act with respect." She turned to face one of the senior board members, a white male, and continued:

"For example, Hank, I have asked you several times not to touch my dreadlocks. You have ignored me and continue to touch my hair. This is not being respectful of me or my requests."

A deafening silence filled the room until Hank started to retaliate by making defensive statements.

What happened next was remarkable. Board members stepped in, saying that this situation was exactly the kind of interaction they needed to work on. They began to talk candidly with one another and even addressed the issues that had caused the friction in months past. All members were engaged, participating and listening to each other.

By the end of the meeting, a trusting atmosphere prevailed. The directors even began to relax and have some fun. They discussed what it would look like to practice **Connected** and **Dependable** behaviors. Before the session ended, they created a Trust Code, which was to serve as a guide to help them maintain their newfound trusting climate during future board meetings.

Did the ABCD Trust Model™ cause this breakthrough? Or was it simply the fact that there was a safe process to guide a critical discussion among highly competent and capable adults who needed a vehicle to resolve their conflicts?

More important than the answer was the outcome. Everyone left exhausted but pleased. Several board members confessed that they'd dreaded coming to the meeting but were thankful it had achieved so much. Some were so relieved that the long-standing atmosphere of distrust had been broken, they were moved to tears. Even Hank and Monique smiled, thanked each other, and ended the meeting with a hug.

Trust works!

Appendix

How Trustworthy Do
You Think I Am?

On the following page are some statements about
my behaviors. Thinking about my behavior in a
specific job or role, please indicate how often you
see me engage in each of the listed actions by
circling one response (H, S, O, V, or A) that best
describes my behavior. I invite you to be candid.
The value of this assessment depends entirely on
your willingness to respond openly and honestly to
the statements.

H = Hardly ever
S = Sometimes
O = Often
V = Very often
A = Always

ABLE
DEMONSTRATE COMPETENCE AND SKILLS

1. Get quality results   H S O V A
2. Solve problems   H S O V A
3. Am highly skilled   H S O V A
4. Am good at what I do   H S O V A
5. Have relevant experience   H S O V A
6. Use my skills to assist others H S O V A
7. Strive to be the best at what I do H S O V A

BELIEVABLE
ACT WITH INTEGRITY

8. Keep confidences   H S O V A
9. Admit when I am wrong   H S O V A
10. Am honest   H S O V A
11. Avoid talking behind people's backs H S O V A
12. Am sincere   H S O V A
13. Am nonjudgmental   H S O V A
14. Show respect for others   H S O V A

CONNECTED
CARE ABOUT OTHERS

15. Listen well   H S O V A
16. Praise others' efforts   H S O V A
17. Show interest in others   H S O V A
18. Share about myself   H S O V A
19. Work well with others   H S O V A
20. Show empathy for others   H S O V A
21. Ask for input   H S O V A

DEPENDABLE
MAINTAIN RELIABILITY

22. Do what I say I will do   H S O V A
23. Am timely   H S O V A
24. Am responsive to requests   H S O V A
25. Am organized   H S O V A
26. Am accountable for my actions   H S O V A
27. Follow up   H S O V A
28. Am consistent   H S O V A

ASSESSMENT TALLY

DIRECTIONS:

1. Enter the number of H, S, O, V, and A responses from the assessment for each section—A, B, C, and D.
2. Multiply by the number indicated and enter your result.
3. Add the results of each box to determine your total score for each section.

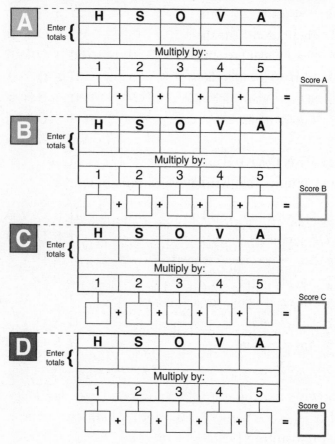

Acknowledgments

To begin, we'd like to acknowledge all the special people over the years who have shown us—through their *Able* deeds, *Believable* words, *Connected* conversations, and *Dependable* actions—what trust looks like. These family members, parents, teachers, coaches, and friends are too numerous to name in their entirety, but this book would have been impossible to write without them.

Cindy extends her sincere gratitude to Nancy Jamison and Lu Olney for their committed focus in helping to develop the initial trust model. She thanks her children—David, Stephen, Jennifer, Debbie, and Catherine—and her eleven grandchildren for their continual support and for teaching her life's lessons of trust. She thanks her husband, George, for personifying trust and believing in and sharing her journey. And for showing her the importance of creating a language of trust, she thanks all the individuals throughout her consulting business.

Martha thanks Henry Ferris of William Morrow for his wry wit, expert editing, and generous encouragement. She thanks Richard Andrews for his sage counsel and representation. And for her sunny smile and editorial camaraderie, she thanks Renee Broadwell.

Ken extends his heartfelt gratitude to Randy Conley, our TrustWorks!™ champion, for his feedback and encouragement. He's also grateful to Margery Allen for her impeccable management of his daily schedule. He thanks his wife, Margie, for her powerful modeling of loving trust. For showing him new dimensions of the power of trust, he thanks his children, Scott and Debbie, his grandchildren, Hannah, Atticus, Kurtis, Kyle, and Alec—and his dog, Joy. Finally, for showing him an example of perfect trust, he thanks Jesus.

About the Authors

Ken Blanchard

Few people have impacted the day-to-day management of people and companies more than Ken Blanchard. A prominent, gregarious, sought-after author, speaker, and business consultant, Ken is universally characterized by his friends, colleagues, and clients as one of the most insightful, powerful, and compassionate people in the business world today.

From his phenomenal bestselling book, *The One Minute Manager* (coauthored with Spencer Johnson)—which has sold more than thirteen million copies and remains on bestseller lists—to the library of books coauthored with outstanding practitioners—*Raving Fans, Gung Ho!, Leadership and the One Minute Manager, Whale Done!*, and many others—Ken's impact as a writer is extraordinary and far-reaching.

Ken is the chief spiritual officer (CSO) of The Ken Blanchard Companies, an international management training and consulting firm that he and his wife, Dr. Marjorie Blanchard, founded in 1979 in San Diego, California. He is also cofounder of the Lead Like Jesus ministry, an organization committed to helping people become servant leaders around the world. He is also a visiting lecturer at his alma mater, Cornell University, where he is a trustee emeritus of the board of trustees. The College of Business at Grand Canyon University in Phoenix, Arizona, bears his name.

Ken and Margie, his wife of fifty years, live in San Diego. Their son, Scott, and daughter, Debbie, hold key positions in The Ken Blanchard Companies.

Ken graduated from Cornell University with a doctoral degree in educational leadership and a bachelor's degree in government. He holds a master's degree in sociology from Colgate University.

Cynthia Olmstead

Dedicated to helping organizations resolve conflicts and achieve success, Cynthia Olmstead founded TrustWorks Group, Inc., in 1987 and served as its president until the firm was purchased by The Ken Blanchard Companies in 2010.

As an organizational development expert, Cynthia recognized that at the core of many problems was the lack of trust—in the organization's direction, in other team members, in leadership. Drawing from her group facilitation and organizational management background, Cynthia developed the TrustWorks!™ program to teach leaders and teams proactive ways to manage conflict, improve communication skills, and build a culture of trust. The program has been successfully implemented in major corporations worldwide.

Earlier in her career Cynthia served as vice president of human resources for a manufacturing firm. She designed and implemented corporate training programs, performance management programs, and appraisal systems. A former employee of The Ken Blanchard Companies, she taught Situational Leadership® II for a decade before establishing her independent consulting practice.

Cynthia graduated from Pomona College with a bachelor's degree in sociology and did postgraduate work at California American University.

Martha Lawrence

A former editor for Simon & Schuster and Harcourt Publishers, Martha is an executive editor at The Ken Blanchard Companies, where she works closely with Ken Blanchard on book projects. Her passion is creating books that encourage the development of people's highest potential.

Over the course of her career she has edited more than one hundred books, including the blockbuster bestsellers *Feel the Fear and Do It Anyway* (published in 1987 and still in print today) and *The One Minute Entrepreneur* (a #1 *New York Times* bestseller in 2007).

Prior to joining The Ken Blanchard Companies, Martha wrote an award-winning series of mystery novels featuring private investigator Elizabeth Chase. The author of numerous short stories, she occasionally writes for the *San Diego Union-Tribune* and *San Diego Magazine*.

Martha graduated from the University of California at Santa Cruz with a bachelor's degree in American studies and did postgraduate work at the New School for Social Research in New York City.

Services Available

The Ken Blanchard Companies® is committed to helping leaders and organizations perform at a higher level. The concepts and beliefs presented in this book are just a few of the ways that Ken, his company, and Blanchard International—a global network of world-class consultants, trainers, and coaches—have helped organizations improve workplace productivity, employee satisfaction, and customer loyalty around the world.

If you would like additional information about how to apply these concepts and approaches in your organization, or if you would like information on other services, programs, and products offered by Blanchard International, please contact us at:

The Ken Blanchard Companies
World Headquarters
125 State Place
Escondido, California 92029
United States
Phone: +1-760-489-5005
E-mail: International@kenblanchard.com
Website: www.kenblanchard.com

United Kingdom
The Ken Blanchard Companies UK
Phone: +44 (0) 1483 456300
E-mail: uk@kenblanchard.com
Website: www.kenblanchard.com/E-mail/?vlc=28

Canada
The Ken Blanchard Companies Canada
Phone: +1 905 829-3510
E-mail: Canada@kenblanchard.com
Website: www.kenblanchard.com/E-mail/?vlc=5

Singapore
The Ken Blanchard Companies Singapore
Phone: +65-6775 1030
E-mail: Singapore@kenblanchard.com
Website: www.kenblanchard.com/
contact/?vlc=200

Australia
Blanchard International Australia
Telephone: +61 2 9858 2822
E-mail: Australia@kenblanchard.com
Website: www.blanchardinternational.com.au

India
Blanchard International India
Telephone: +91-124-4511970
E-mail: India@kenblanchard.com
Website: www.blanchardinternational.co.in

Ireland
Blanchard International Ireland
Phone: +353 879614320
E-mail: Ireland@kenblanchard.com
Website: www.blanchardinternational.ie

New Zealand
Blanchard International New Zealand
Phone: +64 (0) 27 510 5009 / 0800 25 26 24
E-mail: Newzealand@kenblanchard.com
Website: www.blanchard.co.nz

Join Us Online

Visit Blanchard on YouTube

Watch thought leaders from The Ken Blanchard Companies in action. Link and subscribe to Blanchard's channel and you'll receive updates as new videos are posted.

Join the Blanchard Fan Club on Facebook

Be part of our inner circle and link to Ken Blanchard on Facebook. Meet other fans of Ken and his books. Access videos, photos, and get invited to special events.

Join Conversations with Ken Blanchard

Blanchard's blog, HowWeLead.org, was created to inspire positive change. It is a public service site devoted to leadership topics that connect us all. This site is nonpartisan, secular, and does not solicit or accept donations. It is a social network, where you will meet people who care deeply about responsible leadership. And it's a place where Ken Blanchard would like to hear your opinion.

Ken's Twitter Updates

Receive timely messages and thoughts from Ken. Find out the events he's attending and what's on his mind @kenblanchard.